Landmarks of world li

Benito Pérez Galdós

FORTUNATA AND J

Landmarks of world literature
General Editor: J. P. Stern

BENITO PÉREZ GALDÓS

Fortunata and Jacinta

HARRIET S. TURNER

University of Nebraska-Lincoln

CAMBRIDGE
UNIVERSITY PRESS

PUBLISHED BY THE PRESS SYNDICATE OF THE UNIVERSITY OF CAMBRIDGE
The Pitt Building, Trumpington Street, Cambridge, United Kingdom

CAMBRIDGE UNIVERSITY PRESS
The Edinburgh Building, Cambridge CB2 2RU, UK
40 West 20th Street, New York NY 10011–4211, USA
477 Williamstown Road, Port Melbourne, VIC 3207, Australia
Ruiz de Alarcón 13, 28014 Madrid, Spain
Dock House, The Waterfront, Cape Town 8001, South Africa

http://www.cambridge.org

First published 1992
First paperback edition 2004

A catalogue record for this book is available from the British Library

Library of Congress cataloguing in publication data

Turner, Harriet S.
Benito Pérez Galdós, Fortunata and Jacinta / Harriet S. Turner.
   p.   cm. – (Landmarks of world literature)
ISBN 0 521 37262 3 hardback
1. Pérez Galdós, Benito, 1843–1920. Fortunata y Jacinta.
I. Title.   II. Series.
PQ6555.F73T87   1992
863´.5 – dc20   91-40089   CIP

ISBN 0 521 37262 3 hardback
ISBN 0 521 37868 0 paperback

To James Ross Turner
In memory

Contents

Acknowledgments

In preparing this volume, I wish to thank his Excellency Pedro Ortiz Armengol, former Spanish Ambassador to the Philippines, for permission to reproduce and revise, in translation, the charts that preface his edition of *Fortunata and Jacinta* (1979). Observations on the social and historical contexts of the novel gained immensely from his knowledge of nineteenth-century Spain. I am indebted also to Galdós scholars Robert H. Russell, Stephanie Sieburth and Gonzloa Sobejano for their comments; also to the good counsel of Donald L. Shaw, László Scholz, Valeria Wolff, Sarah Swenson and Betty Shull. Oberlin College provided support for the work of research assistants John Marcy, Alice Harris, Elizabeth Spikol and Gregory Romero, with secretarial help from Bernadette Hogan and computer service from Chester Andrews and John Hickey, and no acknowledgment is complete without the remembrance of the cultivated spirit, intelligence and hospitality of doña Carmen de Bourgón Aparici, of Madrid, and her family.

Particularly I am grateful for the encouragement of my children, Henry and Sarah, and for the guidance of J. P. Stern.

Parts of Sections 2 and 3 are based on articles in *Hispanic Review*, 51 (1983) and *Anales galdosianos*, XX (1986). I am grateful for permission to reprint them in revised form. The chapter heading "Metaphors of mind" comes from Michael S. Kearns's book, *Metaphors of Mind in Fiction and Psychology* (1986), and I am indebted to Geoffrey Ribbans for information about the manuscript of *Fortunata y Jacinta*. I have used Francisco Caudet's readily available, annotated edition (Madrid, 1983) of *Fortunata y Jacinta* and all page numbers refer to this edition. My translations are based on Lester Clarke's (London, 1973) and the accomplished version of Agnes Gullón (Athens, GA, 1986).

ix

Abbreviations

References to Galdós's other writings are to the six-volume Aguilar edition of the *Obras completas*, ed. Federico Carlos Sáinz de Robles (Madrid, 1966). The following abbreviations refer to works cited; in the case of several items by one author, the date appears in parentheses in the text of this study. Other references appear in the notes and Guide to further reading.

AC   Americo Castro, *An Idea of History*, Columbus, 1977

AG   Agnes M. Gullón, "The bird motif and the introductory motif: structure in *Fortunata y Jacinta*," *Anales galdosianos* 9 (1974), 51–75

         trans. "Introduction" to *Fortunata and Jacinta*, Athens, GA, 1986, xi–xxii

BPG   *Benito Pérez Galdós, Ensayos de crítica literaria*, ed. Laureano Bonet, Barcelona, 1990

ER   Eamonn Rodgers, *Pérez Galdós, Miau*, London, 1978

         From Enlightenment to Realism. The Novels of Galdós, 1870–87, Dublin, 1987

GR   Geoffrey Ribbans, "Contemporary history in the structure and characterization of *Fortunata y Jacinta*," *Galdós Studies*, vol. I, ed. J.E. Varey, London, 1970, pp. 90–113

         Pérez Galdós, Fortunata y Jacinta, London, 1977

JK   John W. Kronik, "Galdosian reflections: Feijoo and the fabrication of Fortunata," MLN 97 (1982), 272–310

JM   José F. Montesinos, *Galdós*, 3 vols., Madrid, 1968–72

JPS   J.P. Stern, *On Realism*, London, 1973

LB   Lucille V. Braun, "The novelistic function of Mauricia *la Dura* in Galdós's *Fortunata y Jacinta*," *Symposium* 31 (1977), 277–89

MH   Monroe Z. Hafter, "Ironic reprise in Galdós's novels,"
      PMLA 76 (1961), 233–39
MN   Michael Nimetz, *Humor in Galdós*, New Haven, 1968
NV   Noël M. Valis, "El *flin-flán* de la novela: Leyendo
      Fortunata y Jacinta," ABC (1987), 10–11
POA   Pedro Ortiz Armengol, *Apuntaciones para 'Fortunata
      y Jacinta'*, Madrid, 1987
RC   Raymond Carr, *Spain, 1808–1975*, Oxford, 1982
SG   Stephen Gilman, *Galdós and the Art of the European
      Novel: 1867–1887*, Princeton, 1981

Chronology

	Life and works of B. Pérez Galdós	Literary, political and cultural events Spain (Europe)
1843	Galdós is born in Las Palmas, Canary Islands	Sainz del Río and Krausism; Isabella II comes of age
1857	Secondary education (Las Palmas)	Flaubert's *Madame Bovary*; Baudelaire's *Les fleurs du mal*
1859		Darwin's *The Origin of the Species*; African War (Spain vs. Moroccan Empire)
1862	Registers as a law student, University of Madrid	Hugo's *Les Misérables*; Bismarck comes to power in Prussia
1865	Reporter for *La Nación*	Prim's conspiracy; student riots on St. Daniel's Eve;
1866		Revolt of the Sergeants
1867	First trip to Paris	Marx's *Das Kapital* (v. 1); Ibsen's *Peer Gynt*
1868	Translates Dickens's *Pickwick Papers*	September Revolution; Isabella II leaves for France
1870	Writes *La Fontana de Oro* and for *Revista de España*	Deaths of Bécquer and Dickens; Amadeo of Savoy becomes king of Spain; dogma of papal infallibility; assassination of General Prim; envelope in general use (Spain)
1871	Publishes *La Fontana de Oro, La sombra, La novela en el tranvía,* and *El audaz;* father dies.	Bécquer's *Rimas;* Zola's *Les Rougon-Macquart;* Darwin's *The Descent of Man;* Eliot's *Middlemarch;* Amadeo of Savoy arrives in Spain

1872	Editor, *Revista de España*; works on *Trafalgar*, his first *Episodio nacional*	Third Carlist War; sewing machine in use in Spain
1873	Publishes volumes in first series of the *Episodios nacionales*	King Amadeo abdicates; First Republic proclaimed; Cantonalist uprisings in Alcoy, Cartagena, Andalucía
1874	*Cádiz*	Alarcón's *El sombrero de tres picos*; Valera's *Pepita Jiménez*; Pavía's coup after Castelar's defeat in Parliament
1875	Finishes first series and begins the second series of the *Episodios*	Nuñez de Arce's *Gritos de combate*; Alfonso XII begins his reign
1876	*Doña Perfecta*	The *Institución Libre de Enseñanza* founded in Madrid
1877	*Gloria*	Spanish edition of Darwin's *Origin of the Species*
1878	*Marianela; La familia de León Roch*	Edison and Swan invent the electric lamp; Tolstoy's *Anna Karenina*; Alfonso XII marries María de las Mercedes
1879	Publishes second series of the *Episodios nacionales*	Pereda's *De tal palo, tal astilla*; Alfonso XII marries Ma. Cristina of Habsburg-Lorena
1881	*La desheredada*	Echegaray's *El gran galeoto*; Ibsen's *Ghosts* and James's *Portrait of a Lady*
1882	*El amigo Manso*	Stevenson's *Treasure Island*
1883	*El Doctor Centeno* and *Marianela*; becomes European Correspondent for *La Prensa* (Buenos Aires)	Pardo Bazan's *La cuestión palpitante*; Nietzsche's *Thus Spake Zarathustra*
1884	*Tormento, La de Bringas* and vol. 1 of *Lo prohibido*	Nuñez de Arce's *La pesca*; Clarín's *La Regenta* (vol. 1)
1885	*Lo prohibido* (vol. 2); *trip to Portugal* with Pereda	Pereda's *Sotileza* and Clarín's *La Regenta* (vol. 2); Alfonso XII dies; regency of María Cristina

1886	Elected a liberal deputy to Parliament for Guayama (Puerto Rico); begins *Fortunata and Jacinta*	Pardo Bazán's *Los pazos de Ulloa*; Zola's *Germinal* and Tolstoy's *The Death of Ivan Ilyich*
1887	Publishes *Fortunata and Jacinta* and the short stories of *Celín, Trompiquillos* and *Theros*; mother dies	Pardo Bazán's *La madre naturaleza*; Strindberg's *The Father*, 1887, 1897 Jubilees of Queen Victoria
1888	*Miau*	Strindberg's *Miss Julie*
1889	*La incógnita* and *Realidad; Torquemada en la hoguera*; visits Stratford-on-Avon	International Exposition of Paris; Tolstoy's *The Kreutzer Sonata*; Calle de Fuencarral murder trial
1891	*Angel Guerra*	Socialism propagated in Spain; Cánovas returns
1892	Performances of *Realidad* or *Tristana*	Rubén Darío brings Modernism to Spain
1893	Moves to "San Quintín" house in Santander; staging of *La loca de la casa* and *Gerona; Torquemada en la cruz*	Zorrilla dies
1894	Performance of *La de San Quintín* and *Los condenados; Torquemada en el purgatorio*	D'Annunzio's *The Triumph of Death*; Kipling's *The Jungle Book*; the Dreyfus Affair in France (1894–1904)
1895	*Torquemada y San Pedro; Nazarín; Halma.* Performance of *Voluntad*	Pereda's *Peña's Arriba*; Fontane's *Effi Briest*; the Cuban War of Secession
1896	Staging of *Doña Perfecta* and performance of *La fiera*	Proust's *Les plaisirs et les jours*; separatist agitation in the Philippines
1897	*Misericordia* and *El abuelo*; made a Member of the Spanish Royal Academy	Ganivet's *Idearium español*; Unamuno's *Paz en la guerra*; Cánovas assassinated
1898	Writes third series of the *Episodios nacionales*	Ganivet's *Los trabajos del infatigable creador Pío Cid*; Spanish American War and the end of the Spanish overseas empire

1900	Publishes third series of the *Episodios*	Freud's *The Interpretation of Dreams*; Bergson's *Le rire*
1901	Staging of *Electra* (Madrid) — a resounding political event	Freud's *The Psychopathology of Everyday Life*; Mann's *Buddenbrooks*; Queen Victoria dies
1902	Performance of *Alma y vida*	Valle-Inclán's *Sonatas*; Chekhov's *Three Sisters*; Alfonso XIII comes of age
1903	Staging of *Mariucha*	First flight of the Wright brothers; Machado's *Soledades*; James's *The Ambassadors*
1904	Staging of *El abuelo*	Russo-Japanese War
1905	*Casandra*; staging of *Bárbara* and of *Amor y ciencia*; suffers attack of hemiplegia	Einstein proposes his Theory of Relativity; Darío's *Cantos de vida y esperanza*; Unamuno's *La vida de don Quijote y Sancho*
1907	Elected Republican deputy to Parliament for Madrid; publishes fourth series of the *Episodios nacionales* and *Zaragoza*, a lyric drama	Joyce's *Chamber Music*; Machado's *Soledades, galerías y otros poemas*; Maura's "long government" begins
1908	Staging of *Pedro Minio*	Cubist art (Gris, Picasso, Braque); Benavente's *Señora Ama*
1909	*El caballero encantado*	Blériot flies over the English Channel; Marinetti's Futurist Manifesto
1910	Re-elected deputy to Parliament for Madrid; staging of *Casandra*	First student residence created (Madrid); Mexican Revolution begins
1911	Denounces Spanish military measures in Morocco	Baroja's *El árbol de la ciencia*
1912	The Spanish Royal Academy denies Galdós its support for the Nobel Prize; publishes *Cánovas*, last *Episodio* of the unfinished fifth series	Machado's *Campos de Castilla*; Hispano—French agreement on the protectorate of Morocco

1913	Galdós becomes blind; staging of *Celia en los infiernos*	Unamuno's *Del sentimiento trágico de la vida*; Proust's *Du côté de chez Swann*
1914	Staging of *Alceste*	Joyce's *Dubliners*; First World War – Spain is neutral.
1915	*El tacaña Salomón* and *Marianela* staged	Joyce's *Portrait of the Artist as a Young Man*
1916	Staging of *Santa Juana de Castilla*	First World War ends
1920	4 January: Galdós dies in Madrid	E. Pardo Bazán dies

Chronological table of main events in *Fortunata and Jacinta*

1869	October	Maximiliano begins university studies in school of pharmacy
	December	Juan and Fortunata meet (he is 21)
1870	January	Juan and Fortunata consummate their relationship; Amadeus of Savoy takes the throne (2 January)
	May	Juan abandons Fortunata
	June	29th: Juan to Plencia
	July	Juan and Jacinta meet in Plencia
	September	Juan in Madrid
	October/November	First son of Fortunata and Juan born
	December	30th: mother of Jacinta dies
1871	January	Fortunata leaves Madrid with Juárez el Negro; is dragged to and from market places and trade fairs till May
	March	31st: Guillermina soliciting money for her orphanage
	May	3rd?: Juan and Jacinta marry
	June	3rd: Juan and Jacinta return from honeymoon
1872	May	son of Fortunata and Juan dies in Madrid
	July	Fortunata in Lérida and Barcelona
1873	February	10th: abdication of Amadeus of Savoy; 11th: Republic proclaimed
	April	23rd: government in crisis
	May	Juan tires of Jacinta
	July	Juan Pablo Rubin in Carlist headquarters
	December	Ido's "new novel" – the *Pituso* episode
1874	January	3rd: coup d'état; 5th: Fortunata reappears; 19th: Maximiliano meets Fortunata; 21st–22nd Maximilano and Fortunata set up their household (through November)
	April	9th: Fortunata to convent
	June	4th: Fortunata glimpses Jacinta in the convent
	August	Episode of the mouse and the bottle of cognac
	September	29th: Fortunata leaves convent
	October	1st: Fortunata and Maximiliano marry; 3rd: Fortunata renews her affair with Juan

	November	Juan beats up Maximiliano; Fortunata flees
	December	30th: Sagunto's coup d'état; Rubín family moves to Ave María Street
1875	January	14th: Jacinta finds out about Juan's renewed liaison; 15th: Juan walks out on Fortunata
	February/March	Fortunata's interlude with Feijoo
	April	1st: Fortunata is returned to Maximiliano; 12th: Fortunata and Maximiliano reconciled
	May	13th: Fortunata and Jacinta meet and clash while visiting the ailing Mauricia; 15th: Mauricia dies; 25th: Juan and Fortunata renew their liaison for the third time
	June	(through November): Maximiliano grows increasingly mentally unstable
	September	20th: Juan returns from vacation
	October	7th: Manuel Moreno-Isla dies
	November	15th: Juan engineers the breakup with Fortunata
	December	8th: Maximiliano threatens the maid with a knife; 20th–21st: final flight of Fortunata
1876	February	20th: Ballester visits Fortunata
	March	15th: Maximiliano tries to discover Fortunata's whereabouts; 20th: Alfonso XII completes northern campaign against the Carlists
	April	12th: Juan Evaristo, 2nd son of Juan and Fortunata, born; 14th or 15th: Estupiñá confirms the child's legitimacy; 16th: Maximiliano informs Fortunata of Juan's new affair with Aurora; 17th: Fortunata assaults Aurora; 18th: Fortunata bequeaths her child to Jacinta; 19th: Fortunata dies; 28th: Maximiliano to the asylum

Genealogical tables

Table 1   The Trujillo family

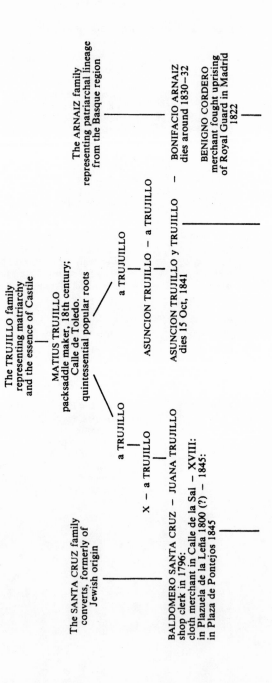

The SANTA CRUZ family
converts, formerly of
Jewish origin

The TRUJILLO family
representing matriarchy
and the essence of Castile

The ARNAIZ family
representing patriarchal lineage
from the Basque region

MATIUS TRUJILLO
packsaddle maker, 18th century;
Calle de Toledo.
quintessential popular roots

a TRUJILLO

a TRUJILLO

X – a TRUJILLO

ASUNCION TRUJILLO – a TRUJILLO

BALDOMERO SANTA CRUZ – JUANA TRUJILLO
shop clerk in 1796;
cloth merchant in Calle de la Sal – XVIII:
in Plazuela de la Leña 1800 (?) – 1845:
in Plaza de Pontejos 1845

ASUNCION TRUJILLO y TRUJILLO   –
dies 15 Oct, 1841

BONIFACIO ARNAIZ
dies around 1830–32

BENIGNO CORDERO
merchant fought uprising
of Royal Guard in Madrid
1822

Table 2   The Moreno family

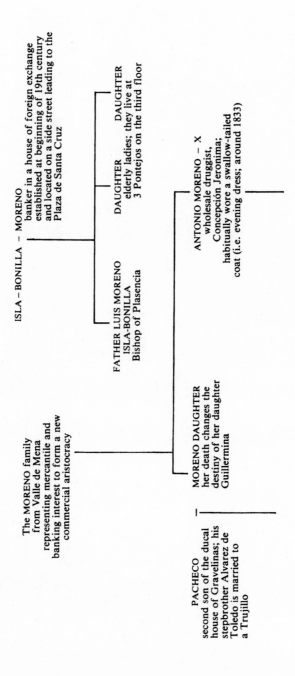

The MORENO family
from Valle de Mena
representing mercantile and
banking interest to form a new
commercial aristocracy

ISLA – BONILLA – MORENO
banker in a house of foreign exchange
established at beginning of 19th century
and located on a side street leading to the
Plaza de Santa Cruz

FATHER LUIS MORENO
ISLA-BONILLA
Bishop of Plasencia

DAUGHTER
elderly ladies; they live at
3 Pontejos on the third floor

DAUGHTER

ANTONIO MORENO – X
wholesale druggist,
Concepción Jeronima;
habitually wore a swallow-tailed
coat (i.e. evening dress; around 1833)

MORENO DAUGHTER
her death changes the
destiny of her daughter
Guillermina

PACHECO
second son of the ducal
house of Gravelinas; his
stepbrother Alvarez de
Toledo is married to
a Trujillo

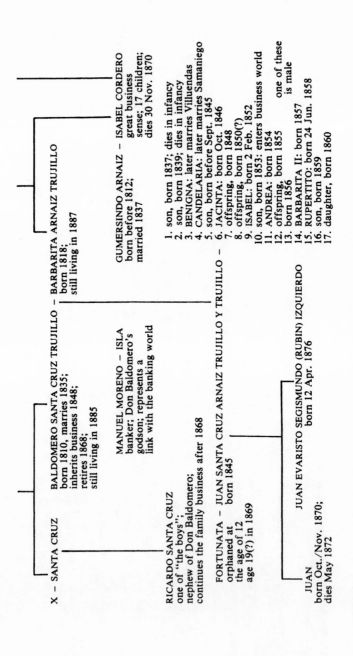

X – SANTA CRUZ

BALDOMERO SANTA CRUZ TRUJILLO
born 1810, marries 1835;
inherits business 1848;
retires 1868;
still living in 1885

BARBARITA ARNAIZ TRUJILLO
born 1818;
still living in 1887

ISABEL CORDERO
great business
sense; 17 children;
dies 30 Nov. 1870

GUMERSINDO ARNAIZ
born before 1812;
married 1837

MANUEL MORENO – ISLA
banker; Don Baldomero's
godson; represents a
link with the banking world

1. son, born 1837; dies in infancy
2. son, born 1839; dies in infancy
3. BENIGNA: later marries Villuendas
4. CANDELARIA: later marries Samaniego
5. son, born before Sept. 1845
6. JACINTA: born Oct. 1846
7. offspring, born 1848
8. offspring, born 1850(?)
9. ISABEL: born 2 Feb. 1852
10. son, born 1853: enters business world
11. ANDREA: born 1854
12. offspring, born 1855
13. born 1856
14. BARBARITA II: born 1857
15. RUPERTITO: born 24 Jun. 1858
16. son, born 1859
17. daughter, born 1860

one of these
is male

RICARDO SANTA CRUZ
one of "the boys";
nephew of Don Baldomero;
continues the family business after 1868

FORTUNATA – JUAN SANTA CRUZ ARNAIZ TRUJILLO Y TRUJILLO
orphaned at
the age of 12   born 1845
age 19(?) in 1869

JUAN EVARISTO SEGISMUNDO (RUBIN) IZQUIERDO
born 12 Apr. 1876

JUAN
born Oct./Nov. 1870;
dies May 1872

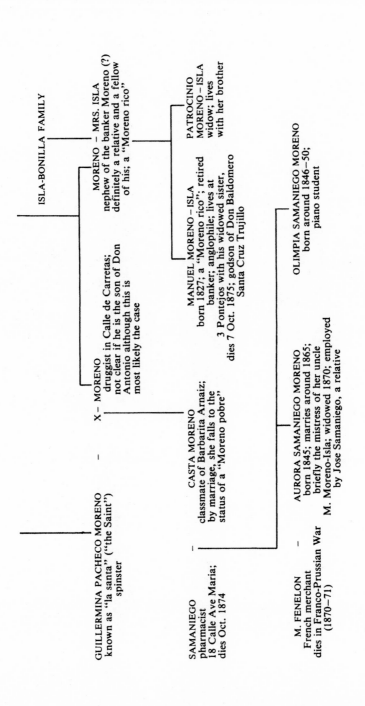

ISLA-BONILLA FAMILY

GUILLERMINA PACHECO MORENO
known as "la santa" ("the Saint")
spinster

X – MORENO
druggist in Calle de Carretas;
not clear if he is the son of Don
Antonio although this is
most likely the case

MORENO – MRS. ISLA
nephew of the banker Moreno (?)
definitely a relative and a fellow
of his; a "Moreno rico"

MANUEL MORENO – ISLA
born 1827; a "Moreno rico"; retired
banker; anglophile; lives at
3 Pontejos with his widowed sister,
dies 7 Oct. 1875; godson of Don Baldomero
Santa Cruz Trujillo

PATROCINIO
MORENO – ISLA
widow; lives
with her brother

SAMANIEGO
pharmacist
18 Calle Ave Maria;
dies Oct. 1874

CASTA MORENO
classmate of Barbarita Arnaiz;
by marriage, she falls to the
status of a "Moreno pobre"

OLIMPIA SAMANIEGO MORENO
born around 1846–50;
piano student

M. FENELON
French merchant
dies in Franco-Prussian War
(1870–71)

AURORA SAMANIEGO MORENO
born 1845; marries around 1865;
briefly the mistress of her uncle
M. Moreno-Isla; widowed 1870; employed
by Jose Samaniego, a relative

Table 3   Marriage alliances of Casarredonda

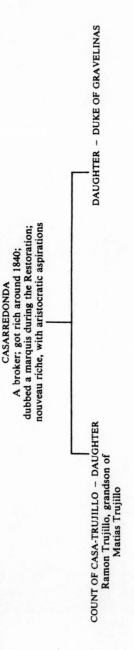

CASARREDONDA
A broker; got rich around 1840;
dubbed a marquis during the Restoration;
nouveau riche, with aristocratic aspirations

COUNT OF CASA-TRUJILLO – DAUGHTER
Ramon Trujillo, grandson of
Matias Trujillo

DAUGHTER – DUKE OF GRAVELINAS

Table 4 The Bonilla family

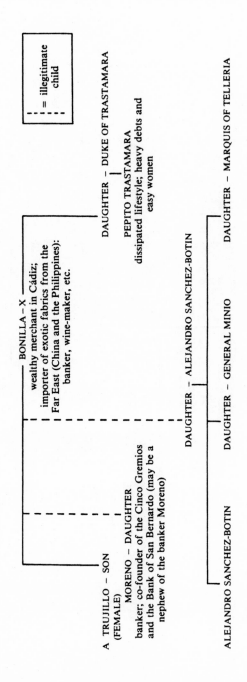

Table 5   The Muñoz and Villuendas families

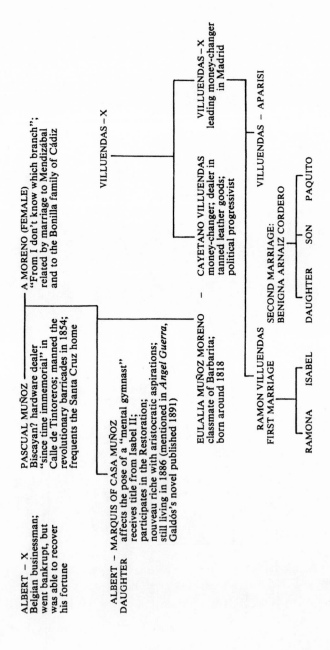

ALBERT – X
Belgian businessman;
went bankrupt, but
was able to recover
his fortune

PASCUAL MUÑOZ
Biscayan? hardware dealer
"since time immemorial" in
Calle de Tintoreros; manned the
revolutionary barricades in 1854;
frequents the Santa Cruz home

A MORENO (FEMALE)
"From I don't know which branch";
related by marriage to Mendizábal
and to the Bonilla family of Cádiz

VILLUENDAS – X

ALBERT – MARQUIS OF CASA MUÑOZ
DAUGHTER   affects the pose of a "mental gymnast"
            receives title from Isabel II;
            participates in the Restoration;
            nouveau riche with aristocratic aspirations;
            still living in 1886 (mentioned in *Angel Guerra*,
            Galdós's novel published 1891)

EULALIA MUÑOZ MORENO
classmate of Barbarita;
born around 1818

CAYETANO VILLUENDAS
money-changer; dealer in
tanned leather goods;
political progressivist

VILLUENDAS – X
leading money-changer
in Madrid

VILLUENDAS – APARISI

RAMON VILLUENDAS
FIRST MARRIAGE

SECOND MARRIAGE:
BENIGNA ARNAIZ CORDERO

RAMONA   ISABEL

DAUGHTER   SON   PAQUITO

Table 6   The Rubin family

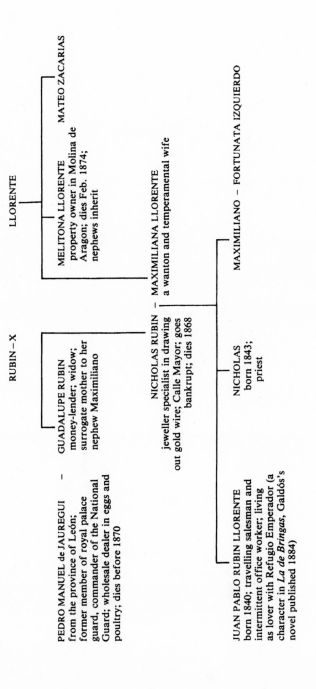

LLORENTE

MELITONA LLORENTE
property owner in Molina de
Aragon; dies Feb. 1874;
nephews inherit

MATEO ZACARIAS

MAXIMILIANA LLORENTE
a wanton and temperamental wife

RUBIN–X

GUADALUPE RUBIN
money-lender; widow;
surrogate mother to her
nephew Maximiliano

NICHOLAS RUBIN
jeweller specialist in drawing
out gold wire; Calle Mayor; goes
bankrupt; dies 1868

PEDRO MANUEL de JAUREGUI   –
from the province of León;
former member of royal palace
guard, commander of the National
Guard; wholesale dealer in eggs and
poultry; dies before 1870

MAXIMILIANO – FORTUNATA IZQUIERDO

NICHOLAS
born 1843;
priest

JUAN PABLO RUBIN LLORENTE
born 1840; travelling salesman and
intermittent office worker; living
as lover with Refugio Emperador (a
character in La de Bringas, Galdós's
novel published 1884)

Introduction

Benito Pérez Galdós (1843–1920)

A few photographs, or the portraits by Joaquín Sorolla (1894, 1911), show Benito Pérez Galdós as a plain man, rumpled in dress, his face distinguished only by a curling moustache and sly look. His hands hold a cigar or cane; a scarf trails down his overcoat or a cat lies curled on his lap. Even formal portraits have an informal air – Galdós looks ordinary, much like his friend Máximo Manso, protagonist of *El amigo Manso*, 1882, who sits stroking a cat to conceal his unease. Plainness, reticence, an ironic smile – these traits seem at odds with Galdós's prodigious literary achievement: seventy-seven novels, fifteen original plays and numerous occasional pieces, written between 1867 and his death in 1920. At least a dozen of his contemporary social novels rank with the best in any language.

Galdós was born in 1843 in Las Palmas, Canary Islands, the last of ten children. He started out modestly enough, leaving home and a domineering mother at the age of nineteen to study law at the University in Madrid. But he hardly attended classes. Café life, the theater and events of a city in political turmoil claimed his attention. In 1867, though still registered as a student, he made a first trip to Paris, discovered Balzac and, as he says, "breakfasted" on the novels of *La Comédie Humaine*. From Balzac he conceived the idea of writing a series of interrelated historical and social novels, seeing himself as a writer, not a lawyer, and started *La Fontana de Oro* (*The Golden Fountain Café*), his first full-length novel. He completed it in France the following year, and translated Dickens's *Pickwick Papers* from a French version (1868) before returning to Madrid in 1869 to work as a reporter. The next year was decisive for Galdós's career: he joined the

1

editorial staff of *La Revista de España* and wrote a book review, titled "Observaciones sobre la novela contemporánea en España," which contains one of his most comprehensive statements about the art of the novel. He also published a perplexing psychological novel called *La sombra* (*The Shadow*), followed by fiction in an opposite vein, the historical novel *El Audaz* (*A Reckless Man*, 1871).

The decade of the 1870s established the pattern for Galdós's later productive life as a novelist, playwright and newspaperman, as he sought to blend journalism, drama and prose fiction. Articles written on the stage, travel, literature, art, opera, music, biography, education, politics, crime, current events, social types and customs became grist for plots. Accounts of the crimes of the day read like detective stories, and commentaries on the maneuvers of politicians reappear in the "mental gymnastics" of characters like Manuel Peña (*El amigo Manso*) or Jacinto Villalonga. All these writings transformed their respective genres, provoking debate and public interest in the historical and contemporary social novel.

While current fiction offered no suitable Spanish models upon which to build, Galdós's early novels and newspaper articles bear the impress of *costumbrismo*, a literary genre that flourished in the 1830s in Madrid, as shown in the sketches and articles of Ramón de Mesonero Romanos (1803–82) and Mariano José de Larra (1809–37). In Andalucía an interest in native mores gave rise to the regional novel of Cecilia Böhl de Faber (*La Gaviota*, 1849), Alarcón (*El sombrero de tres picos*, 1874) and Valera (*Pepita Jiménez*, 1874). On the Cantabrian coast, in Santander, José María de Pereda, a Catholic conservative opposed to Galdós's liberal views, wrote of life in mountain and fishing villages (*Sotileza*, 1886), while further west in Galicia, the countess Emilia Pardo Bazán (*Los Pazos de Ulloa*, 1886) trained her eyes on the French and Russian novel. In Oviedo, ancient capital of Asturias, Leopoldo Alas ("Clarín") forsook *costumbrismo* for more symbolic and satiric modes, writing his two-volume masterpiece *La Regenta* (1884–85) in the manner of Flaubert and Zola.

Costumbrismo as practiced by the observant, genial Mesonero Romanos consisted of *cuadros* — picturesque sketches of social types and customs of Old Madrid. Galdós saw the novelistic possibilities of such *cuadros*, and in *Fortunata and Jacinta* he pays homage to his old master by inventing the colorful figure of Plácido Estupiñá, born, the narrator tells us, in the same year as Mesonero (1803). Galdós also relies upon the interaction of narrator and character, illustrated to perfection by another *costumbrista*, the Romantic ironist Larra. In his celebrated sketch of "El castellano viejo" (1832), defined as a stolid, chauvinistic type, Larra becomes the object of his own critique. A reluctant guest at Braulio's dinner party, Larra, impeccably dressed in a pearl-gray suit, dons the enormous, ill-fitting jacket of his host, sips from a wine glass sullied by greasy lips, accepts a bite from the fork of his black-toothed neighbor and receives in his lap a shower of spilled gravy. Nor can he avoid performing at table, declaiming verses, "vomiting" silliness, acting out the role of *castellano viejo* more vehemently than his host.

The sketch depicts an important tension in Spanish cultural and intellectual life, registered as the conflict between the influence of things French and the reaffirmation of a popular, conservative culture. This tension, present in Spanish life since the ascent to the throne of Philip of Anjou, Louis XIV's grandson, in 1713, was exacerbated at the start of the nineteenth century by the Napoleonic invasion (1808) and the War of Independence. In "El castellano viejo" Larra gives that tension a particular ironic twist. As narrator he casts himself in the role of an educated man, French in manner and literary taste, who succumbs to the backward, native ways of his host and emerges somewhat chastened, even enlightened, by those ways, though he voices an acerbic critique and seeks refuge in the hypocrisies of an elite group that looks to Paris for inspiration. In effect, the cultural dissonance felt between France and Spain appears to have shaped something new in Larra's sketch, something distinctively novelistic that is bound up with the reciprocity between narrator and character. Here the roles of narrator and character momentarily stand reversed as Larra, a Frenchified man of letters, acts like his host, while the bawling Braulio displays a native vitality, quintessentially Spanish (*castellano*), which Larra recognizes as the more authentic.

Galdós, who understood the irony of sketches like "El castellano viejo," recalls the dinner party scene in *El amigo Manso*, and recasts Larra as the aloof, aristocratic expatriate Moreno-Isla in *Fortunata and Jacinta*. He recalls also those mixed feelings of fascination and resentment which, as Rodgers notes (ER, 1987), marked the influence of French culture in Spain. In Part 1, his narrator, a social historian attached to the folkways of Old Madrid, takes particular care to document the invasion of French styles of dress, architecture and administrative practices, and characterizes the Frenchified tastes of Juanito Santa Cruz and Aurora Fenelón as unhealthy, even treacherous. Also like Larra, Galdós appears to slip in and out of the text, slyly observing and telling from within his own novelistic world. Dozing in an armchair on a stifling afternoon, he lets a character rap him to wakefulness with a fan. Sitting in a café, he listens to stall sellers, civil servants, defrocked priests, gun runners, students, soldiers, moneylenders and ladies of shady reputation. In a bedroom, he observes a married couple, cutting cinematographically from one face to another as the rhythms of thought and interest command. But unlike Larra, always a moralizer, Galdós maintains an illusion of transparency, not encumbering the social novel with critiques and opinions. Everything appears to pass through his mind effortlessly, even distractedly, and in this we discern a kind of porousness about his sensibility. Galdós appears like a man who absorbed essences and expelled them as *novelas* while he observed or participated in the politics of the day. For him, writing was as easy as "drinking a glass of water," said Clarín, who marveled that Galdós on occasion wrote as many as four novels a year.

The impression of naturalness in writing, however, owes as much to Galdós's preoccupation with narrative technique as to temperament. When he studied works by other European writers, notably Dickens, in order, as he says, "to catch them at their craft," or when he spoke of the difficulty of attaining a natural tone, complained about the disadvantages of third person narration or, like Henry James, became convinced that scenic art achieved more realistic affects than narration in his own voice, Galdós displays an almost modern post-Flaubertian self-consciousness about his art. In his prologue to the 1901 edition of *La Regenta*, he acknowledges Clarín's innovations, and the influence of *La Regenta* marks aspects of characterization in *Fortunata and Jacinta*.

However, in the 1870s and 1880s, as Rodgers observes, Galdós established the modern realist novel in Spain virtually single-handed. He provided an example to younger writers like Clarín, fostered a climate of critical opinion hospitable to the serious social novel, and reconceived the genre as a network of stories told by the characters themselves, either as first-person narrators or in dialogues or monologues that a more or less omniscient narrator retells within finely worked patterns of interrelatedness. While the descriptions of social scenes and character types abound in *Fortunata and Jacinta*, every important stylistic device acquires a larger function; facts, cited in a casual manner, work as thematic motifs, causing the most ordinary of things to incite extraordinary events, feelings, perceptions or states of mind. Within a system of realistic representation, psychological and moral complexities appear to be breathtakingly simple, and this, in a nutshell, is why *Fortunata and Jacinta* is a Landmark among the great works of nineteenth-century European realism.

Galdós's novels divide into two main categories: the historical and the contemporary social. The forty-six historical novels, called *Episodios nacionales* ("Episodes in a Nation's Life"), make up five series, each consisting of ten interconnected novels, except the fifth series, which was left unfinished. Beginning with *Trafalgar* (1873), which depicts the rout at sea in 1805 of the combined fleets of France and Spain by the British navy under Nelson, the *Episodios* chronicle military, political and social events of the century up to the Bourbon Restoration and the 1880s. The first two series of the *Episodios* (twenty novels) appeared in a mere six years, between 1873

and 1879. These treat events preceding the War of Independence against Napoleon and the war itself. A rapid pace,
an eye-witness protagonist who recurs throughout each series,
and the drama of explosive events — these kept the public
enthralled.

The remaining series of twenty-six novels, published between
1898 and 1912, carry the reader through a maze of political
and social events from 1834 to 1879 — Carlist Wars, palace
intrigues, the revolution of 1868 and overthrow of Queen
Isabella, the brief reign of Amadeo of Savoy, the aborted
First Republic and the Bourbon restoration (Alfonso XII).
In the main, these events correspond to the historical background of *Fortunata and Jacinta*. All told, the *Episodios*
were written in two periods, near the beginning and the end
of Galdós's career, bracketing, as it were, the contemporary
social novels. Simply the chronology of Galdós's works shows
how history and fiction appear to contain each other. In
Fortunata and Jacinta, the historical novel and the notion
of history-turned-story within a novel do become as one,
sketching out a meta-fictive dimension within the mimetic
mirror. This interior duplication shows Galdós's basic affinity
with Cervantes and the painter Diego de Velázquez, whom
he cites as precursors of the modern Spanish realist novel.

The thirty-one contemporary social novels, published
between 1870 and 1915, also divide into two groups: *Las
novelas de la primera época* (1870–79) and *Las novelas
de la serie contemporánea* (1881–1915). The novels of the
early period comprise Galdós's first attempts at novel-writing,
as well as four so-called "thesis" novels: *Doña Perfecta*
(1876), much admired by the American writer and editor
William Dean Howells, the sequel *Gloria* (1876–77), *Marianela*
(1878) and *La familia de León Roch* (1878–79). As Rodgers
(1987) observes, Galdós's initial approach was shaped by
the belief, coming from the Enlightenment, that ingrained
social and religious prejudices had blocked progress in Spain.
Literature has a crucial role to play in educating the reading
public, altering individual consciousness to lay the groundwork for national regeneration. Thus Galdós, an avowed

realist, saw the novel as having primarily a social and moral purpose, a view in which he persisted to the end of his career.

While it appeared to early critics that Galdós affirmed substance over form, his concern with the instructional potential of narrative led to another, opposite consideration – how to reconcile ideology and realism in the contemporary social novel. To Galdós's eye, the tension between substance and form, between morality and mimesis, was only apparent. He knew that didactic effects depended for their success upon technique, upon the ways ideas were presented narratively. He knew he must strive to create in fiction the illusion of reality so that the reader would confuse the two, applying to life outside the novel the values imaged within. In his famous early essay of 1870 ("Observaciones ...") he spoke of fiction's power to absorb the reader, drenching his senses in lifelike impressions, thereby to convince us that if life presents novelistic experiences, a novel by Cervantes or Dickens appears as more real, that is, as more authentic, more truthful in every particular than life itself.

The power of a novel to shape the way people seek to interpret their own experience blurs boundaries between author and narrator, character and reader. A recognition of this power determined Galdós's own narrative technique. At the same time, in the manner of Cervantes, the power of literature over the human mind became a chief, didactic concern, the unifying theme of almost his entire literary production. Why, he had asked in 1870, was there no modern Spanish realist novel? Spain had always shown a liking for the real – witness Cervantes and Velázquez – whereas nowadays the contemporary "truthful novel" has been supplanted by French imitations. As he says, evasion marks our restless times; the reading public cries out either for the nostalgia of archaic folkways (*costumbrismo*) or for serialized romance and salon fiction, modeled on Dumas and Soulié – "pale traitors with a sinister look, angelic seamstresses, whores with hearts of gold, wayward duchesses, romantic hunchbacks, adultery, extremes of love and hate" (BPG, 107). These images represent clichéd ways of thinking, seductively set against the grist of ordinary life. As a populist, conservative writer, at odds with the influence of things French in Spain, Galdós inveighs against such fictions, which at best distract, at worst corrupt, by pandering to the wish for identifiable conflicts and easy solutions.

And yet Galdós's own overriding aim in the series of contemporary social novels was to make fiction seem as unlike fiction as possible, with characters so familiar and yet so problematic that in them we recognize ourselves, with settings and scenes so skillfully narrated and dramatized that we feel compelled to exclaim, as Matthew Arnold did of Tolstoy's *Anna Karenina*, that this is the way life is: "The author has not invented and combined it, he has seen it; it has all happened before his inward eye, and it was in this wise that it happened ... The author saw it all happen so − saw it, and therefore relates it; and what his novel in this way loses in art it gains in reality." Like Tolstoy, Galdós invents a narrator who relates as he sees or listens, acting in the story as a reliable witness, reliability giving rise to realism in novelistic form. At the same time, contriving an appearance of the real approximates his narrator's approach to the novel-making imagination of unreliable characters like Isidora in *La desheredada*, doña Cándida in *El amigo Manso*, or Juanito Santa Cruz. These characters persist in mistaking *novelas* for the way life is, half-consciously ministering to their own appetites and desires − Isidora becomes self-orphaned as she imagines her origins as a serialized romance; doña Cándida, aping the social text, serves up rancid wine as champagne, stringy beef as *filet à la Maréchale*; Juanito, on the prowl for Fortunata, invents a new role for himself as a "father" or "brother" who combs the city for a lost, beloved "child." He does not realize how his thinking mimics the way characters behave in those Spanish imitations of French salon fiction.

The potential for irony in such analogies determined Galdós's preoccupation with the popular novel. Now, as in the *Quijote*, literature itself becomes central to plot as novels, librettos, letters, newspapers, magazines and administrative jargon shape speech and behavior. Why and how the shaping takes place, as well as the use people make of images, matter as much as their ostensible meaning. The power of the mind to think, feel and imagine, as well as the question of why people do so and to what effect, become the acts that make up the news, *noticias*, which Galdós intends to tease out of society's solid stuff as *materia novelable*, as declared in his speech to the Spanish Royal Academy. The crux, then, of what is real in the "truthful" modern Spanish novel is bound up not with naming the thing, in the manner of the *costumbristas*, or evading it in favor of the ready-made image, as in the *feuilleton*, but with naming the feeling aroused by the thing, particularly living things, as these appear to pass through individual minds.

Américo Castro, recalling a term of don Sem Tob, a Jew in fourteenth-century Spain, calls this kind of naming "*la fazienda*" – the "inner doing" of consciousness, that is, "what we are to do with ourselves and with the world of things and people who at once enter into us and among which we all evolve." Castro applies the concept to the *Quijote*, showing how outer action (*vivienda*) becomes inner action that is something the mind keeps making (*fazienda*). This "inner doing" of a particular spirit creates those criss-crossing story-lines of Cervantes's great novel, which after two centuries comes to influence sketches like Larra's as well as the nineteenth-century European realist novel. As Castro points out, the *Quijote* is manifestly the origin for Stendhal's *The Red and the Black* (1830) as it is for *Fortunata and Jacinta*. Cervantes, then, is the direct precursor of Galdós's contemporary social novel.

The process of "inner doing" starts in *La sombra* (187,), Galdós's first novel, gathers speed in his little story about a novel overheard in a trolley car (*La novela en el tranvía*, 1871), and refuels, as it were, through the double narrative energy of *Doña Perfecta* (1876), a study in religious fanaticism. As an allegory, that is, as a thing described *under* the image of another, *Doña Perfecta* presents a self-reflecting world of made-up words: on occasion, the narrator slips into his own story and adopts unawares the narrative strategies of doña

Perfecta herself, spying, eavesdropping, mimicking speech. Unexpectedly, the "inner doing" of the narrator stands in approximate analogy to this particular character, as each makes novelistic efforts to impress avid "readers" both within and without the text. Even in the early novels, then, what is real appears to rest more upon the "inner doing" of perception than an easy faith in mirrored facts, while the clichéd intensity of serialized romance and salon fiction appears also to turn inward, passing through commonplaces of daily life (*vivienda*) so that these appear invented (*fazienda*).

How Galdós combines fact and fiction to subtler effect in his next group of novels represents what he called his "segunda manera." *Fortunata and Jacinta* occurs midway among the novels of this second group, initiated in 1881 by *La desheredada* and rounded off by *Misericordia*, published the same year (1897) as Galdós's speech to the Spanish Royal Academy. Three lesser novels followed, representing a return to a more abstract allegorical mode, although Galdós always adhered to the concept of balance as part of his theoretical equation for realism. He maintained that fiction, an image of life, is *in fact* life the way it is, and that novels are neither faithful mirrors nor pure invention but something in between, something simultaneously real ("*vivienda*") and invented ("*fazienda*"). Always, he says, in creating a realist novel, a "perfect point of balance should exist between exactitude and beauty."

Fortunata and Jacinta (1886–1887)

Galdós's masterpiece in four parts was written in eighteen months, from January 1886 to June 1887. The main action of the plot begins with the opposition of the two women and ends with their reconciliation. Part 1 (eleven chapters, representing events between December 1869 and February 1874) starts with the story of Jacinta. The narrator presents Juanito Santa Cruz, only son and heir. He gives the genealogy of the Santa Cruz-Arnáiz alliance, recounts the marriage of Juan's parents, don Baldomero and Barbarita, and depicts the young man's encounter on the stone staircase with Fortunata, a plebeian girl of Old Madrid. Barbarita arranges the marriage of her son to his first cousin, Jacinta Arnáiz. On the honeymoon, Jacinta wrests details of the story of the affair from her husband, learns of Fortunata's pregnancy and abandonment, recognizes a wrong done, and starts thinking obsessively about her rival. Two years pass, and since no children are forthcoming in the marriage, Jacinta attempts to adopt *el Pituso*, a child she believes is Fortunata's, not knowing the child had in fact died. Juan puts a stop to the plan, hears of Fortunata's return to Madrid, and sets out in pursuit.

Part 2 (seven chapters, from February 1874 to autumn) tells Fortunata's story. The narrator introduces the Rubín household, headed by the entrepreneurial doña Lupe who lives with her nephew, Maximiliano Rubín, an intermittently disturbed young pharmacist who meets Fortunata after her affair with Juanito, falls in love and proposes marriage to redeem her. Doña Lupe, scandalized but with an eye for the girl's great beauty and docile ways, sends her to Las Micaelas, a convent for wayward women. There the girl renews her acquaintance with Mauricia *la Dura*, a demented "bad" woman of the streets, who nudges her toward the trap Juanito has prepared by renting rooms next to the apartment Fortunata and Maxi will occupy after the wedding. In Las Micaelas, Fortunata also sees Jacinta for the first time and becomes obsessed by her. Once discharged from the convent, Fortunata marries Maxi but immediately falls into the trap, living in adultery with Santa Cruz. Maxi discovers the affair and Fortunata leaves him.

Part 3 (seven chapters, from the end of 1874 to June 1875) presents the confrontation of Fortunata and Jacinta. Juanito Santa Cruz has discarded his mistress for the second time. A retired military man, Evaristo Feijoo, takes Fortunata under his protection and arranges a reconciliation with Maxi. The restoration of both marriages coincides with the restoration of the Bourbon dynasty as King Alfonso XII enters Madrid. Mauricia *la Dura*'s death in a tenement house sets Fortunata and Jacinta face to face. Guillermina, a religious social worker, intervenes, both women feel betrayed, and Fortunata resolves to conceive another child in order to substantiate her claim as Juan's rightful wife in contrast to the childless Jacinta.

Part 4 (six chapters, from June 1875 to the following spring, 1876) Galdós orchestrates the reconciliation of Fortunata and Jacinta. Maxi, suspecting anew his wife's infidelity, goes mad, and Ballester, head pharmacist, tries to calm him. He too falls in love with Fortunata, who in turn has confided her affair to Aurora, daughter of the owner of the pharmacy. Aurora, employed in a new boutique across from the Santa Cruz house, insinuates to Fortunata that Jacinta is having an affair with Moreno-Isla, a rich bachelor and family friend. The supposition is false, although Moreno is desperately in love with Jacinta. She recognizes but repudiates his suit and Moreno dies. Now Fortunata, again pregnant, returns to la Cava, her place of origin, and gives birth to the child as Juan takes up with Aurora. Maxi discovers the treachery and attempts to "assassinate" Fortunata with the news; she, in turn, grips an iron key, marches into the boutique and slaps Aurora senseless. The ensuing struggle brings on a hemorrhage, but as she dies Fortunata bequeaths the child to Jacinta. Now Jacinta imagines a reconciliation with her rival and sees Moreno as the father of the child. Santa Cruz becomes a stranger to his house and Maxi, aware of his own madness, enters an insane asylum.

While the plot is relatively straightforward, Galdós uses a complex range of narrative perspectives that cause the stereotypes of *costumbrismo* and serialized romance to "enter" particular individuals and incite their "inner doing"; now the received *fact* of a stereotype becomes the first term of his theoretical equation (*exactitud*), counterpoised to new, fictional images (*belleza*). If, in 1870, Galdós had inveighed against the clichés of Frenchified serial romances, we find these clichéd character types re-imaged in new ways in *Fortunata and Jacinta*: those "pale traitors with sinister looks" resurface in Aurora's treachery; "whores with hearts of gold" determine in part the characterization of Mauricia *la Dura*; "angelic seamstresses" reappear in the angel-faced Jacinta, but also in Fortunata, who strives for respectability as she learns to use a Singer sewing machine and dies a self-declared "angel"; finally, emotionally charged thoughts, typical of "romantic hunchbacks," bubble as "fermented jealousy" in the deformed Maximiliano Rubín. In this way, the "rub" (*fazienda*) between prefabricated images and new aesthetic forms lets us discover how the obvious (*vivienda*) is in fact extraordinary.

The same dialectic determines the novel's genesis, recalled thirty years after publication in Galdós's memoirs and titled "Remembrances of an Unremembering Writer" (1916). He tells how, upon returning to Madrid, his friend and fellow novelist, don José Ido del Sagrario, appears at the door. Ido tells of the characters abandoned by their author over the summer. This account moves Galdós to action: rambling through Old Madrid, waving, talking, listening, copying, he points to a stall-keeper who is the spitting image of old, parrot-faced Estupiñá, a character type so familiar that no description is warranted. What is real, then, seems simple, straightforward and natural.

The scene, however, depicts two novelists and two stories, each reflecting the other to confound our notion of the real. Galdós writes a novel that contains Ido's own novel, the imagined episode of the child Jacinta tries to adopt in Part 1. And in that episode, which unexpectedly finds a real counterpart in the child Fortunata gives Jacinta, Estupiñá, apparently interchangeable with a real person, ends up running counter to type — we really do not know him at all. What is this? Both author and character appear to be out of their heads, "gone from the Sanctuary," as Ido's name implies. Thus the easy opposition of fact and fiction is stood on *its* head, since Ido's news becomes a fact that restarts a story, while the author becomes a character, slipping into his own novelistic world. In the alternating action of one and the other we discern the expansion and contraction of a living lung, for as summer "expires," a stopped story starts, and Madrid's social *pulmón* appears to take a breath in the remembered moment of the genesis of *Fortunata and Jacinta*.

In sum, Galdós saw the contemporary social novel not as

a "thing" or even a book but, in the first instance, as something alive, as "*natural*" as breathing, and as an agent of perception. Naming and narrating are mimetic gestures that represent facts, known types, accuracy in detail, and represent the first term of his theoretical equation. The second term, represented by a figure of speech or structural image, refers to aesthetic form. What is real emerges as a consequence of the dialectic between these two terms, as a word, event, person or thing passes through perception to become an image. Thus whatever affects a person's consciousness and moves it to action is represented by certain imagistic progressions. Within these progressions, an "inner doing" particular to the individual starts to take place, manifested in the way something inert becomes animated − like the chalice in Mauricia *la Dura*'s dream, Maxi's piggy bank, or the hairs that bustle about the "balconies" of Nicolás's nose and ears. What is crucial, as in the case of a chalice that starts glowing, staring and speaking, is not the representation of fact or form but the transformations that happen in between, as facts pass through an individual's consciousness and become images. As Galdós's narrator tells the two entwined stories of married women, attention shifts from the description of objects or the way characters perceive them to that notion of a balance maintained between the one and the other. The achievement of this balance, then, accounts for the novel's intense impression of life-likeness, for its "ilusión de vida," to recall the words of Menéndez y Pelayo, Spain's polymath of the nineteenth century, who endorsed Galdós's entrance into the Academy.

At the time of publication, however, few readers understood the range and depth of the dialectical realism of *Fortunata and Jacinta*. Nor did critics perceive how Galdós had adapted Cervantine irony and the mechanism of "interior duplication" to pose anew the problem of character autonomy and the capacities and limitations of the imagining mind. Galdós himself, wary of an adverse reception, went abroad when his four-part novel appeared in June 1887. In his absence Clarín sent an open letter to the newspaper *El Globo*, noting the author's evasion in a sketchy review that, quite ironically, appears to parody its own censure. The novel is too long, too dense, too digressive, he says, and Galdós's ear for commonplace speech undoes the dramatic tension that builds within certain scenes. A more focused approach, in the style of the Goncourt brothers, as well as substantial deletions, are necessary – get out your red pencil, Clarín tells Galdós, while he himself rambles around central points and appears to rely more on hearsay than on a close reading of the text.

Yet Clarín's letter persists as the most insightful contemporary review of *Fortunata and Jacinta*. He emphasized the extraordinary mimetic aspects of the novel, noting how the two stories of married women emerge from commonly known, believable facts of the social life of the times – money, social class, cultural institutions, contemporary politics and private life. Nor did Clarín flinch at what other readers considered of questionable taste, even immoral – the novel's intimations of sexual feeling and behavior. He also understood the relationship Galdós established in *Fortunata and Jacinta* between scrupulously observed details and deeper aspects of character portrayal, and Clarín confirms how, in certain descriptions, observation itself gave way to something else, to a kind of inkling (*"adivinación"*) or stroke of genius. He found this genius best displayed in the extreme behavior of Mauricia *la Dura* and in the appearance of minor characters like *Papitos* or the little hunchbacked nun, Sor Marcela.

Other, more Modernist critics like Valle-Inclán, Unamuno and Ortega y Gasset paid attention only to what they saw as the excesses of a copyist, and censured Galdós for his obsession with the boring buttoning and dressing of daily life and his lack of "style." Valle-Inclán's sneering epithet "Don Benito el Garbancero" summed up their case: Galdós was a writer fit only to write about a plate of beans (*garbanzos*). This attitude cost Galdós a nomination for the Nobel Prize in 1912 and came about, in part, because as a novelist he himself had made the cultivation of simplicity, of a "non-style" in speaking, dressing and writing, a cherished, major theme. For example, in *Tormento* (1884), the narrator states that style is a way of lying, whereas truth stands staring and silent ("El estilo es la mentira. La verdad mira y calla").

Clarín's review, however, offered the insight that in *Fortunata and Jacinta* style and substance are one and the same. In effect, the very notion of character, once established as "fact," appears as *passed through* formal elements of style and structure. Thus what Galdós called "character" emerged as a constellation of bits and pieces, as something "evented," while events became "personed," imbued with personality, to recall Américo Castro's words for what happens to character in the *Quijote*. "Style," therefore, becomes fundamental to the impression of life-likeness in the novel, and Clarín spoke admiringly of Galdós as a "naturalist," a term he took to mean "realist" rather than to refer to the French school of naturalism.

In his review, Clarín warned also of the envy of fellow novelists. Unamuno, who felt that envy with particular sharpness, persisted to the end in his negative view of Galdós's "style," even when his own novels, like *Niebla* (1914) and *La tía Tula* (1921), owed much to experimental interior monologues, as well as a pronounced interest in feminine psychology, which *Fortunata and Jacinta* displays. The poet Federico García Lorca, however, was a fervent admirer of Galdós, and declared in 1935, one year before his death, that Galdós "sounded the truest, most profound voice of modern Spain" (SG, 287). For Lorca, the word "modern" meant a daring, imaginative capacity, manifested precisely in Galdós's style. For as the narrator relies increasingly on figurative speech in *Fortunata and Jacinta* metaphors appear not only to capture the essence of what is real but also to encapsulate Galdós's theoretical equation, conjoining what is represented with a notion of how representation is achieved. In effect, far from eschewing "style," Galdós saw metaphor itself as an organizing principle of thought and action, and created images not so much to depict a particular mind but to show, as did Cervantes, how people *use* their minds, and to distinguish and evaluate those uses, which in the main correlate with a hierarchy of parts in both the individual and social body. Galdós's metaphors pick out *viscera* in the plebeian Fortunata, whose convictions arise, as she says, from deep within herself ("de *entre* mí"), *sleights of hand* in Santa Cruz, who plays with the "dice cups of reason" and *imagination* in Maxi, whose thinking correlates explicitly with the operations of metaphor.

In this way, Galdós's theoretical equation not only implements the creation of his novelistic world, but also functions through metaphor as a constituent part of the two stories of married women. The equation represents both a means and an end, a process and a theme, which is nothing less than the problem of interpretation itself. In the present volume, an analysis of the closing scene of Part 1 illustrates this phenomenon of self-referentiality in Galdós's novel and explicates the relation of metaphor to truthfulness and lying, to right and wrong. This interrelatedness gives rise to the dialectical realism of *Fortunata and Jacinta*, specifying a richness and complexity that Modernist critics could not see in "don Benito el garbancero" − a man of rumpled dress, cane in hand, who appeared able to write only about a plate of beans.

Chapter 1

Social and historical contexts of a changing world

History, politics and private life

The events of *Fortunata and Jacinta* take place some fifteen years prior to the time of writing and publication, from September 1869, when Juanito first meets Fortunata, to her death in late April 1876. The ancestry of the Santa Cruz family reaches back to the eighteenth century and beyond, originating in a primal blood-tie between female cousins of the Castilian Trujillo clan. The matriarchal line establishes the trunk of the great family tree, while matriarchy and monarchy, alternating with the Republic, determine a reciprocity between history, politics and private life. The alternations correspond to the pervasive, acute state of imbalance that marked Spain's emergence into the modern period, dated approximately from the Napoleonic invasion in 1808, followed by the "liberal codex" of the Constitution of Cádiz of 1812. A constitutional system was maintained during the periods 1834–68 and 1875–1923, alternating with periods of absolutism and revolution and culminating in the Spanish Civil War (1936–39).

Following the enlightenment and reforms accomplished during the reign of Charles III (1759–88), the nineteenth century in Spain saw, among other conflicts, a sporadic civil war between Carlist factions and the central government in Madrid. Carlism, first as a factious group, then as a military insurgency led by Ferdinand VII's younger brother, maintained divisions throughout the country. Almost a decade (1856–63) of stability was gained by the *Unión Liberal* government of Leopoldo O'Donnell, which, supported by a new prosperity, encouraged foreign investment and expanded the railway system. By 1863, however, the moderate and liberal parties could not agree on a common platform and Queen Isabella allowed parliamentary government to founder, relying exclusively on the personal influence of trusted advisors like O'Donnell and Narváez. The economy went into sharp decline and the Queen herself became a public scandal. Her overblown figure, bulging Bourbon lip, impotent husband and many lovers – the father of her son Alfonso XII was rumored to be an American dentist – incited an era of political chaos.

Galdós, enrolled as a law student at the University of Madrid from 1862 to 1866, witnessed events such as the Noche de San Daniel on 10 April 1865, a student protest against the dismissal of the eminent orator and professor Emilo Castelar, and the "Revolt of the Sergeants" (22 June 1866), in which a military garrison at Madrid declared its support for the progressive leader, General Juan Prim. Both uprisings, ruthlessly suppressed by the government, determined Galdós's life-long defense of liberal causes.

Events closest to the plot of *Fortunata and Jacinta* took place one year after the Revolution of 1868, when the public, disgusted with the Queen and her advisors, supported a revolutionary coalition of liberal progressives led by Juan Prim. Prim pronounced against Isabella, became Prime Minister of the provisional government, and pressed to create a constitutional monarchy. Searching throughout Europe for a king, he found a willing candidate, the Italian Duke of Aosta, who entered Spain as King Amadeo of Savoy on 3 January 1871. Upon arrival, however, the King learned that Prim had been shot in a Madrid street, a catastrophe for the new monarchy and for the revolutionary coalition of 1868. Amadeo abdicated on 11 February 1873 after a brief, stormy reign.

On the day of Amadeo's abdication, the Cortes proclaimed the First Republic; unrest and disillusion only grew worse. Four presidents of the executive *Junta* took office in less than a year. Their task was to transform the First Republic, rife with splinter groups and local insurgencies, into a Federal Republic, constitutionally defined as the legal government of the Spanish people. As the Federal Republicans struggled to contain rebellion in the eastern provinces of Andalusia and Murcia, Castelar and Salmerón continued their personal feud in the capital until 3 January 1874, when Manuel Pavía, Captain General of Madrid, marched into the Cortes, fired a few shots in the air and ended the First Republic. Now an emergent liberal society, attached first to the inept rule of Isabella II, embraced Alfonsism, the movement to restore the constitutional monarchy with Isabella's son Alfonso as king.

Since both Alfonsists and Republicans refused to take part in the national government imposed by Pavía, General Serrano, representing Radicals and Constitutionalists, took over the presidency, sheltering a conspiracy led by a young brigadier, General Martínez Campos. Martínez Campos pronounced against Serrano on 29 December 1874 and proclaimed the return of the Bourbon dynasty, carried to Spain from England in the person of King Alfonso XII, nephew to Queen Victoria (and great-grandfather of Don Juan Carlos, present King of Spain). On 9 January 1875 Alfonso XII entered Madrid, installing the new government of the Restoration under the direction of Cánovas del Castillo. The king and his advisors endeavored to create a two-party system of liberals and conservatives, implementing what came to be known as the *turno pacífico*, the alternation in power of two parties created expressly by government influence that sought to manipulate an uninformed, indifferent electorate. But parties simply formed and dissolved, sometimes ironically by royal decree, and were often in opposition to the monarchy itself. In 1885 King Alfonso died of consumption and, under the Regency of his Habsburg wife, María Cristina, the liberal party headed by Sagasta, who appointed Galdós to Puerto Rico's seat in Parliament, remained in power until 1890.

The years between the revolution of 1868 and the last years of the reign of Alfonso XII correspond to the narrated time of *Fortunata and Jacinta*, since Galdós, in the guise of narrator, makes the time of writing part of the history chronicled in the two stories of married women. The mark of imbalance and instability of those years bites deep into structure and characterization, starting with the opening page when Juanito

Santa Cruz, like Galdós, takes part in the student riots on the eve of San Daniel. The narrator links births, marriages and deaths to historically resonant dates, blending fact and fiction to make his text analogous to the depth and range of contemporary economic and social change. Throughout the nineteenth century this change was a fitful process, not at all uniform but rather like "a fugue in which old voices do not cease to sound when new voices enter" (RC, 2). Old and new voices mix as history goes on parade in the reminiscences of Estupiñá or Jacinta's mother, Isabel Cordero, who is as adept at manipulating birthdates as she is at peeling potatoes.

Isabel's way of associating those "momentous occasions" that marked the reign of her namesake, Queen Isabella II, with the birthdates of her own brood does more than highlight contemporary events in the story. National history is relived as a domestic enterprise – Carlism starts a quarrel at the washbasin between the Rubín brothers; doña Lupe recalls Prim's short-sighted *"jamases"* as he claims *never* to have given way to the monarchy; Guillermina mentions King Amadeo's big mouth and full lips, mimicking his foreign accent as he donates *"gueales"* instead of *reales* to her orphanage. Gossip authenticates fiction as historical fact; fact and imaginative representation merge as we see a national history centered in family, house, street and café.

Thus what Galdós presents as character, self or psychic formation evolves with the rest of history, while juxtapositions between public and private events convey the irony of hindsight. For example, at the beginning of Part 1, the births of Isabel's seventeen children and the non-birth of the Santa Cruz heir stand linked to the political progeny of Queen Isabella and the non-birth of solutions. The coincidences between Isabel Cordero as the "lamb" and Prim, each a "general" who dies "sacrificed" in the line of duty, frame the arranged marriage of the junior Santa Cruzes within the alternation between Monarchy and Republic, and invite the use of the battle metaphor to point to a common adversarial note, as pervasive in relations between men and women as between political factions. Through his friend, the smuggler Estupiñá, the narrator slips in a rapid synopsis of the century, "with its revolutions, its flamboyant generals and futile *pronunciamientos* — all amounting to little more than speeches from a balcony" (GR, 1970, 92). Stupid old Estupiñá, who bustles about the city, heedlessly gossiping, and Isabel Cordero, a wreck of a woman, are figures who do more than initiate parallels between public and private life. They embody traits deeply set in the collective psyche, the foundation of history: in don Plácido, *placidity* — smug self-satisfaction and an opportunistic gift of the gab that masquerades as hard work; in Isabel, martyred motherhood in a society that caters to the masculine prerogative. Her unmarried daughters are viewed as a "plague" and Juan Santa Cruz, asking for Jacinta's hand, enters her home as the Messiah.

History-turned-story

Historical parallels appear to implement Galdós's theoretical equation as he seeks to represent, in times of imbalance, a "perfected equipoise" between Spain's political instability and the fickleness of Juanito Santa Cruz. The entitlements of family history — wealth, privilege, power — cast him in the title role of Part 1. At the beginning of the story, the narrative point of view refracts early events through Santa Cruz family history, using their only son and heir as agent of the action. The monarchy metaphor, religious configurations like the name Santa Cruz (Holy Cross), Juanito's initials J S C, and objects of veneration like the robe and chalice the family sets upon the altar of the convent of Las Micaelas, all work to combine politics, money and religion. These three governing institutions of late nineteenth-century Spain — Church, State and Commerce — stand reflected in the privileges, actions and habits of mind of this young man — "Santa Cruz is like God himself," declares Segunda Izquierdo, Fortunata's scabrous aunt, expressing a veneration that causes Fortunata to take particular pride in her son, "king of the house."

The references to contemporary politics (1869–75) trace the fitful course of Juanito's marriage. The Santa Cruz heir "obeys an impulse for the sake of change," craving novelty, fearing boredom, swinging from wife to mistress as the country alternates capriciously between monarchy and republic (GR, 1970, 97). The mechanics of these swings within idleness correlate to the failure of liberal Spain, since political change, like an engine idling, occurred unaccompanied by social and economic changes which could have given substance to the revolution. Thus in Part 3, when don Baldomero states how the nation reacts, like a child, only to immediate stimuli, oscillating between stable and revolutionary regimes, the narrator applies the idea to Juan. He shows how the vicissitudes of don Baldomero's son, in whose sober progress the father has placed such confidence, mirrors the times. Ironically enough, instability is the one fixed trait of Madrid society in the 1870s, just as it is in Juanito and in the nation at large. The parallels shape a structural image that reiterates familiar themes — a family history inserted within national history, a man attached to contemporary politics who mirrors the times, and the tangible density of family relations — all describe nested structures, infantile attachments, parasitic appetites, and give a sense, within the repetitions of alternating regimes, of no time, memory or change.

Beneath this history-turned-story is the paradox of progress and regress, worked out as the narrator represents the way the family lives. He brings out the paradox in references to don Baldomero's "timid *progresista* affiliations, his "respectability" that solves the problem of Juanito's arrest, his benevolent, patriarchal rule, which dispenses with the adopted child and demands during dinner that Jacinta keep smiling, even when King Alfonso XII's parade brings her the news of Juan's renewed affair. Progress turns to regress as Barbarita applauds the new, boyish King, while the elder Santa Cruz jumps about with the news, as happy as a child with new shoes. Regress colors the placidity of Plácido Estupiñá, who swoons like a schoolboy in Barbarita's presence. It persists within coming of age to cloy conversations in the bedroom between Juan and Jacinta and to prompt Feijoo's remark about civil servants who rush to suckle on the state. In Part 4, doña Casta's preference for water from the *Progreso* canal that supplies the fountain on Pontejos Square sums up the social process: as she rattles off labels on bottled waters − *Progreso-Merced-Pontejos* − the names work backward emblematically, tracing out her particular social decline. Doña Casta had started out a "Moreno-rico," living in a "progressive," well-to-do commercial area near Pontejos Square, but she ends up in cramped quarters on Ave María street, living as a "Moreno-pobre." Now in full, ironic regress, she hoists the *Pontejos* bottle to sample, as by an act of mercy (*Merced*), the illusion of progress by tasting the best (*Progreso*) waters.

In these minute, telling ways, the entwinement of social history, politics and private life depicts an incipient decadence within family and nation. To show how decadence moves within an entrepreneurial society, the narrator exploits the theme of politics selectively, to his own political advantage, as it were, turning the notion of politics itself into a kind of self-sustaining metaphor. An alternating account like Villalonga's report of Pavía's coup deconstructs the latest news, making, as we shall see, a *noticia-novela* that politically manipulates a political event into a fiction that affects both public and private domains. History recedes, stories advance as Galdós conceives the "inner doing" of the story-telling mind as an agent of action − Jacinta prompts her husband to tell Fortunata's name, Fortunata confesses to Guillermina her plan to have a child, and Maxi tells Fortunata of Juan's affair with Aurora. Stories give birth, stories enlighten, stories kill.

Progress and regress in story-telling also affect the narrator; now the "inner doing" of his own coming of age inscribes another *novela* within branching story lines. Toward the end he appears to listen more, conveying thought and action in dramatic scenes in which use of the gerund predominates, almost in the manner of a stage direction. His concern with history becomes less marked in favor of an interest in states of mind, as indicated by his use of poetic figures of speech in the descriptions of the deaths of Moreno-Isla and Fortunata. The narrator invokes this more ahistoric style as a consequence of history. Now he endeavors to catch hold of the real news, the real *noticias*, by affirming feeling and imagination over historical event. The story-telling mind becomes an aesthetic object, and an object of ethical inquiry for Galdós. Thus, by Part 4, parallels between history, politics and private life disappear along with that most historical and political person, the titled Delfín. Santa Cruz, history's showpiece, exits from the novel, while imagination moves to center stage as Jacinta reconstructs the birth of Fortunata's baby and Maxi's mind lives in the stars. Juanito has become but another accident of history; he is now subject to history's own evolution as *fiction*, for in the end his entitlements of privilege within the family count for nothing, while the imagined *novela* of Fortunata's and Jacinta's new baby counts for all.

Family tree and social class

As the title and subtitle suggest, *Fortunata and Jacinta — Two Stories of Married Women* is structured upon the opposition of two social spheres: the slum life of prostitutes, poor people, laborers, artisans and orphaned children (Fortunata, Mauricia *la Dura*, Papitos, the child *Pituso*) and the upper bourgeoisie — mercantile and banking families like Santa Cruz, Moreno-Isla, Ruiz Ochoa, who sit atop the pyramid of power. The two spheres, places at opposite ends of the social spectrum, shade reciprocally into a third, the petty bourgeoisie made up of drifters and disgruntled office-seekers — Juan Pablo Rubín, don Basilio Andrés de la Caña, the tragic Villaamil; households like those of doña Lupe and *las Samaniegas*; the druggist Ballester, and the usurer Torquemada. All three spheres are connected by plot: Juanito Santa Cruz's affair with Fortunata, a working-class girl who eventually marries Maximilian Rubín, doña Lupe's nephew.

The main structural element underpinning plot and motivating in part these indispensable connections is the branching, labyrinthine Santa Cruz family tree. Like the tree (*madroño*), emblem of the city of Madrid, its trunk and branches reach out to every sector of the city, stemming, ever so remotely, from one Matías Trujillo, muleteer and harness-maker on Toledo street, to the exquisite refinement of don Manuel Moreno-Isla, the aristocratic expatriate educated in England and friend of King Alfonso XII. As we have seen, story-telling itself, a rich, polyphonic mixture of gossip, jokes, asides and whispered confessions passed along the Madrid grapevine, twists into an enormous *enredadera*, a running vine, a narrative structure similar to the entwined branches of the tree. The family tree, origin of the trunk of the two stories, also defines their narrative shape, and stands reflected in the archetypal symbol of the tree of life that occurs toward the end of the novel. This correlation of images discloses the full power and range of bloodlines of a family, in which one member's existence becomes linked with the never-ending cycle of life and death. From this remote perspective of human history, a single life like Moreno's shrinks to a dry leaf dropped indifferently from the great tree. Family tree and tree of life coincide, informing the novel with a deep and fundamental ambivalence that links, at the beginning, that primitive Trujillo harness (*aparejo*) to Ballester's perception of good and evil that, as he says, "walk about *yoked together*" (*aparejados*) at the end. Now the notion of a realist novel as a mirror walking along the road encompasses reflections that are moral in value.

The collusion of tree and harness images lends a kind of "beveled edge" to storytelling, casting an ironic shade over perceptions about the source of human sustenance. The great family tree nurtures and starves, embraces and suffocates as it connects lives to universal experience, while indicating patterns of familial closeness, characteristic of Madrid society of the times. Lineage and linkage become dense and ramifying in *Fortunata and Jacinta*. Galdós implants the seeds for the confrontation and reconciliation between the two women in every circumstance, social custom or institution – economic or religious, public or private. Descriptions that trace those *enredaderas* of the family tree burgeon with tiny, dramatic scenes from childhood, adolescence and adulthood – there, in one tendril, is doña Casta ("Castita") Moreno's connection to Barbarita Santa Cruz, in another, to her rich cousin Moreno-Isla, in a third, even more remotely, to Guillermina. This closeness of social connections, of news told animatedly not only by people but also by their possessions, turns the narrator's text into a context for further action. Even cloth and chairs have a story to tell. Now plot becomes almost synonymous with speech, perception and point of view, as relations eclipse action and events. Often the mere mention of a name in varying contexts is enough to attest to the permeability of nineteenth-century Madrid − a bourgeois social body on the move.

Tertulias

Small talk, ritually installed in cafés, classrooms, kitchens and storefronts, gave rise to a time-honored social institution known as the *tertulia* − a specialized kind of group conversation that preceded the advent of clubs and casinos. *Tertulias* start the story from within, at the very hub of history in the making, for this is a society formed and flourishing in speech. Peeping through the iron grillwork fronting on San Cristóbal street, the narrator, a member of the *tertulia* of cloth merchants, spies three chairs in fat old Arnáiz's fabric store. There, small talk has taken a seat as he looks at the animated presence of bentwood chairs, which had replaced a bench with no back, covered with black oilcloth; the predecessor of that bench had been a large chest or empty box.

The three chairs tell the history of the cloth trade, of marriage, money and social class, sketching out in a train of remembrances something of the imprint of those habits of mind that attended the rise of mid-nineteenth-century Madrid's commercial bourgeoisie. Such mental and moral imaginings bear thematic consequences as the two stories of *Fortunata and Jacinta* begin to unfold. The chest, hewn from native wood, speaks for founding enterprise − bolts of cloth made in Spain as opposed to imported textiles. It speaks, too, for small but tenacious bourgeois beginnings, close to folkways, allied from their conception to the monarchy and based on thrift, upon closely guarded, hoarded gains. Work is unremitting, discipline severe: don Baldomero I *el grande* slaps his son for wearing dress clothes on a working day, usually twelve or more hours long, and requires all clerks to drop to their knees to say the rosary with the family every Sunday evening. That heavy chest is also a sign for a materialistic, bureaucratic way of thinking: two generations later, Juanito, heir to the fortune of the Santa Cruz-Arnáiz alliance, *deposits* his thoughts, *packs* them in *boxes*, *draws* upon resources and *inserts* a comment, reifying thought and feeling. On his honeymoon, the sight of Valencia's curving coastline prompts him to *pigeonhole* ideas as one places *things* in a drawer.

The chest sits near the grilled window at the front of the store. Isabel Cordero, wife of Arnáiz's bungling nephew, has an eye for ventures glimpsed beyond that window's iron grid, and she hugs to *her* chest a vision of the very newest fabrics imported from Switzerland, Belgium and France. Crammed with profits, the primitive chest is replaced by a bench, slightly plumped and covered with oilcloth. The covered bench indicates an inch of easement, lighter times, looking toward a financial well-being that finally arrives around the mid-1840s, when Barbarita Arnáiz, now married to Baldomero Santa Cruz, stops in after shopping to join the *tertulia* and catch the drift of conversation between the narrator, Arnáiz, and don Plácido Estupiña. *Placidez* – comfort and complacency – now characterizes family members who sit back in those three chairs, made, we note, not of heavy native wood, like that stolid chest, but of curved, polished wood, in imitation of the Viennese chair.

In *tertulia*, the three chairs tell how a small house active in the cloth trade has become an international business while maintaining a toe-hold in Old Madrid. Around the 1840s, progress is the order of the day: just as chests cede their place to benches and chairs, solid stacks of coins give way to paper bills, gas lighting replaces oil lamps, postage stamps and envelopes speed communication, shop windows, protected by iron grillwork, expand to new, glass-fronted displays, *escaparates* that invite the eye "to escape" into a manufactured foreign realm. People buy imported ready-made clothing. The famous *mantón de Manila*, that flexible shawl, bright with embroidered birds and flowers, no longer reigns. It, too, has given way to buttoned coats, to a feigned sobriety as the aristocracy imitates foreign manners and the middle classes, ever conscious of French fashion as a sign of class distinction and upward mobility, step away from native dress and consign the shawl to gypsies and working-class women. Buttoned coats invade display rooms while the *mantón* lies exiled, packed in boxes in the basement of Arnáiz's store. Railroad, telegraph and steamship have *placed* ("colocado") Madrid within forty-eight hours of Paris, as if the Spanish city were a knick-knack on the shelf of the great French capital.

It is a time when money talks. The disentailment of church lands in 1837, tariff reforms of 1849 and 1868 and the revolution of that same year, which dethroned Queen Isabella II and prepared the way for the aborted reign of Amadeo and the First Republic, all put money into the hands of a rising middle class, creating *nouveaux riches* like the bourgeois speculator José de Salamanca who brought the railways and financed the building of luxurious new houses. Everything is on the rise. Newly rich merchants seek noble titles, like the Marqués de Casa Muñoz, descended from a blacksmith on Tintoreros street and dubbed in haste by the departing Queen Isabella II, or Ramón Trujillo, recently made a count. Arnáiz, remembering the family's common ancestor Matías Trujillo, that inglorious harness-maker of Toledo street, slyly suggests that cousin Ramón cook up a family crest with the inscription that "I" (meaning the harness) "once belonged to Babieca" ("Pertenecí a Babieca") – after all, why *not* upgrade that mangy harness to the reins of Babieca, El Cid's noble steed, taking Trujillo bloodlines back to old Castile, to the very founder of a nation?

Old, pre-industrial Madrid is changing, and in Arnáiz's store the transition from primitive chest to refined chair reflects how an unwashed populace, pot in hand for an infrequent bath, has responded to the construction of a public system of canals, an engineering feat that brought water from the Guadarrama mountains to Madrid on 24 June 1858. Now the city, once represented as a clodhopper dressed in gentleman's clothes or as a galumphing, grimy peasant girl, is becoming a civilized, European capital – clean, tidy and above all *decent*. But the chairs tell, too, of other alterations, scarcely glimpsed through that close fretwork of social decorum and historical progress: a degenerative difference between father and son. Baldomero Santa Cruz, founder of what is construed as a mercantile "dynasty" and known as Don Baldomero I *el grande*, began as a clerk in a cloth store in the 1790s. His son, Don Baldomero II, inherits the business in 1848 and in the main conforms to tradition by expanding the trade, making more money. By 1868, with "net profits of fifteen million *reales* safely stowed away," he retires so that his idle son Juanito may spend the family fortune. And Juanito spends it idly, "sitting" in those chairs, so to speak. The slightly sensual curves of imported wood hint at his preference for European luxury, his taste for Parisian courtesans as opposed to Fortunata's native ways.

Traditional storekeepers talk incessantly. Estupiñá criss-crosses streets like a weaver's shuttle while Arnáiz stays put; together they appear to weave stories on a loom, working warp and woof across, up and down so as to lend emphasis on the connection between the notion of text and textiles. Conversation, like liquor, intoxicates don Plácido, putting him out of business and on to the street where he counts on *relaciones* and affiliation to the Santa Cruz family. *Relaciones* – contacts, friendship, patronage – persist as the most important social expression of wealth, not noble crests nor the snobbery of conspicuous waste (RC, 60). Hence the narrator's insistence on what he views (in Part 1 at all events) as an essentially classless society, as well as the relative modesty of the Santa Cruz entourage – no fancy carriages, no cooks in chef's hats, no social column in the newspaper. Talk is all. As Gilman notes, it is a time of osmosis between printed and spoken language: women read novels, men read the evening paper and both sexes go to the theater. The emphasis is on conversational exchange and journalism, *relaciones* that support a system of electoral bosses like Villalonga, who in Part 3 dispenses a provincial post to Juan Pablo Rubín in return for votes at the local level. Making money and making novels become twin enterprises in the *tertulias* of Old Madrid; even furniture specifies links between history, commerce and culture. In this way, the pieces and parts of *Fortunata and Jacinta* remain bound to one another through a series of connections that depict closeness in society, context for the text we read.

Up the down staircase

Dialectical energies, signposted in title and subtitle, trace out the "social curve" that Fortunata recognizes during her stay in the convent of Las Micaelas, establishing a criss-cross pattern of social interaction. On the one hand, a vast network of stories and events, held together by the "cash nexus," links social spheres, charting the course for the confrontation and reconciliation of Fortunata and Jacinta. On the other, family ties determine a society that moves up and down within contexts that exploit and divide the two women, each living subservient to the dictates of class, money and the masculine prerogative. Galdós starts and ends his story on the great stone staircase. In Part 1, the narrator states how Juanito, on a visit to Estupiñá, carries his particular *novela* up the steps in the same moment that the family declines in vigor. After the encounter, Fortunata rushes down the staircase, answering to her name which someone screeches from below, whereas in Part 4 she goes up the stairs to occupy an apartment at the very top – above even Plácido Estupiñá's quarters. In Old Madrid, upper rooms indicate a lower social order: wealthy families spread out on first floors while poorer relations must climb stairs, taking a perch at the top. Fortunata's story inverts the value of this up-down social order to exert an effect on the narrator. In the beginning, this narrator, heart in mouth, climbed that stair as he sought to tell the history of the Santa Cruz-Arnáiz alliance. At the end, he prefers to let Moreno-Isla, Fortunata, Jacinta and Maxi speak for themselves.

At the beginning, the Santa Cruz family sits enthroned: don Baldomero and doña Barbara are king and queen, Juan and Jacinta, prince and princess, dubbed *el Delfín, la Delfina*. Within Spain's patriarchal society, the matriarchal character of the family is paramount, and in the beginning, as in the end, we feel the bludgeoning effect of that matriarchal Trujillo "steely bar" – Trujillo power, Trujillo will. The formidable mothers Juana and Asunción Trujillo had arranged the founding marriage of don Baldomero Santa Cruz and Barbarita Arnáiz, second cousins to each other. Once a mother, doña Bárbara rules as an enlightened despot, setting up the reign of her only son and heir. His full name – Juanito Santa Cruz Arnáiz *Trujillo y Trujillo* – carries with repetitive linguistic force the sense of that "bar of steel" which takes a new form at the close of Part 4: Fortunata herself, once an outsider but now mother of the only Santa Cruz heir, grips an iron key to assert her own "Trujillo" version of powerfully felt maternal rights, precisely Spanish, by using it to smash in the face of Aurora Fenelón – a sissified French woman ("francesilla") in her eyes, while the virginal Guillermina, as tough as any Trujillo *mamá*, tries to take over as *tutora* of Fortunata's child.

Wealth, privilege and order show how at the top the Santa Cruz family epitomizes social custom, religious orthodoxy. But, from below, Fortunata rises to form a new family, challenging those traditions and social codes. Fortunata's "family" represents a true mixture, however ephemeral, of age, sex and social class. Sitting on the staircase, engaged in a multi-leveled *tertulia*, is Guillermina, followed by Ballester, two steps down, then Maxi, José Izquierdo and finally that croaking hag, Segunda. Fortunata's new family is open, communal, egalitarian. The child, baptized "Juan Evaristo Segismundo" for father, lover, friend, carries in descending order the determining factors of Fortunata's life in a "stepped name"; the name, like the stone staircase, implies an up-down moral order in reverse. Now Fortunata proposes that *three* women share mothering – she, as "la mamá primera," Jacinta as "la mamá segunda," Guillermina as "la mamá tercera." Fortunata gives birth not only to a son and heir but to a new concept of matriarchy and of family.

The stone staircase, owned by Moreno-Isla, inherited by Guillermina, administered by Estupiñá and inhabited by Fortunata, becomes a metonymic spatial image. It sums up the four parts of the story, while depicting a relatively open society, as close in its attachments as the rooftops of old Madrid that appear to catch each other by the hand, as changing as fashion, as informal as a family. The narrator finds it an agreeable society, one that retains diminutives, expresses affection, feels comfortable with the body, respects grief and knows kindness. His narrative manner manifests this familiarity as his mind melts into the consciousness of people *via* the free, indirect style, dialogue and monologue. He has an ear for features of popular speech and the vernaculars of class, while other linguistic features condense emotional closeness: the reiterated use of the ethical dative, possessives in the first person, astonished asides, and adjectives saturated with indulgence like "bendito," "bueno" or "pobre." This narrative tone is part of the social context it describes. It lavishes upon the smallest, most wretched detail the moral quality of *simpatía* – a persuasive, finely calibrated personal warmth, so constant and equitable that it creates an illusion of objectivity; even the most wretched animal enjoys the dignity that this tone conveys. Stuffed in slatted cages, chickens press and peck to stretch a neck for air; here, on the very floor of the chicken shop, waiting in line for the slaughtering machine, birds talk turkey, saying, "hey, you stuck *your* beak out farther than me ... now it's *my* turn to stick my neck out all the way."

This tangible sense of openness and exchange permits a representative of every social class to be seated at the abundant board of the Santa Cruz house. It encourages doña Lupe, in more straitened circumstances, to make alterations to a velvet coat, acquired as a pawned article in payment, so as to hob-nob with Guillermina Pacheco and other high-society ladies. And it sparks a bourgeois consciousness in the minds of poorer housewives like Mauricia *la Dura*'s sister, Severiana, who refers deferentially even to Fortunata as a *señorita*. Severiana, while privileged among the poor, maintains with some struggle her cramped quarters in the tenement house of Mira el Río, but, back from shopping, just like doña Bárbara, she digs into her bag of groceries and exultantly displays broccoli, a nice cut of steak, and eggs. In close proximity, rubbing elbows, one class mimics the other. A suspicion of *socarronería* – that dry, ironic wit characteristic of the narrator – lurks in such behavior as we suspect that doña Lupe's prized acquisition, a velvet coat, may be the luscious blue velvet coat Fortunata is forced to pawn at the close of Part 1. A piece of clothing climbs up and down the social staircase to characterize a fallen woman in terms of another on the rise.

The narrator, taking his seat at the Santa Cruz table, has enjoyed the flattering notion that imitation was a sign of progress and democratic sensibility. How curious to note, he says, that our society, behind the times in so many ways, actually presents quite a happy mix of social classes, each comfortably adjusted to the other. He finds the mixture healthy and modern, and thinks no threat of social uprising is likely to cause trouble, since an attenuated, pleasant sort of socialism already runs in everyone's blood. This rich, respectable and well-connected family provides, like the cloth trade, samples from all spheres. At the table, precisely on Christmas Eve, the narrator looks down the rows of seafood platters and sees the "birth," so to speak, of a whole new nation, nothing less. Here is an upwardly mobile society in which old bloodlines, shown by Gravelinas and Alba, mix with a newly minted aristocracy, like Casa-Muñoz, and shop clerks like Jacinta's brother-in-law, Pepe Samaniego, share space with bankers of prominence like Ruiz Ochoa. Thus the narrator, surfeited with good food, pictures a social body of close, interrelated families, eager to pay homage to talent and enterprise, disdainful of noble lineage – "circumstances of birth mean nothing to us," he says. But class divisions persist and indeed are strengthened by those very family ties that bind things to the status quo. The narrator glosses over differences in upbringing and privilege, making these appear as part of the natural order; hence the myth of classlessness that so pleases him in Part 1.

Yet notwithstanding the "democratic temper of the Spaniard," the narrator does acknowledge that class divisions, determined mainly by money, respond to a kind of Newtonian mechanics – gravitational pulls and laws of motion which have a life of their own. Thus on that Christmas Eve of 1873, the benevolent don Baldomero II brings along to dinner a winning lottery ticket and everyone crowds around to receive a share, backslapping, embracing ... *even the servants*. *La señorita* Jacinta rushes the news to the kitchen, and cook, butcher, coalman and maid, daring for a moment to breach etiquette, peep abashedly, unbelievingly, from the doorway; five wretched little *reales* exploding to three million ... the scullery girl faints from such sudden good fortune. The Santa Cruz house, where supposedly democracy reigns, is founded upon the rock-hard distinction between servant and master, exemplified by don Plácido, whose only reason for existence, as Fortunata notes, is to serve his betters.

The invention of this in-between character in a transitional chapter carries its own conjurer's trick, played out as narrator and character double for one another as social historians, and as the former sketches in the latter an ostensibly familiar type – the old-style storekeeper. But as this family servant runs up and down the staircase, taking a short cut through a Trujillo shoe store or sitting interminably on Arnáiz's chair, recounting events, don Plácido typifies the very opportunism and corruption displayed in the narrator's historical survey of the rise of the bourgeoisie.

Outside, things change; inside, they remain the same. Outside, Estupiñá moves and talks, relates and connects; inside, he speaks for immutable, older ways. Here is a person who makes the sign of the cross where the demolished Church of Santa Cruz used to stand and waves to religious icons as if they were old friends, yet thinks nothing of slipping "underneath" the recitation of the rosary breathless accounts of bargains to be had in the Plaza Mayor. Scrupulously honest with acquaintances, as an occasional smuggler he takes pride in cheating the nation, bribing officials and doing favors for friends. Open and accommodating to a fault, he scorns poor people. The old stone stairway, worthy of a nobleman's castle, is close to his heart – not for him cheap, rickety, wooden steps that "ordinary people" use. Estupiñá's snobbery reaches back to origins – that Trujillo mule harness raised by cousin Ramón to Babieca's reins. In his shop, the complacent don Plácido dismisses rudely the common customer in deference to "ladies of distinction." An old man, he is child-like in his enthusiasm, counting on his fingers or flying kites with Juanito; unmarried and celibate, he is nonetheless "addicted" to Barbarita – flaming glances at Christmas dinner "send arrows" her way, yet as he takes up Barbarita's cause, spying on Juanito during the young man's first affair with Fortunata, loyalty to the "prince" whom he himself had dubbed "the Dauphin" (*Delfín*) makes him an accomplice to sexual exploitation.

Narration and social class

In Part 1, the narrator is quite compromised by the point of view of the upper bourgeoisie. Assembled with others in the comfortable, well-appointed *salón*, he rather smugly contemplates the glossy portrait of don Baldomero I *el Grande* and shows benign but telling social prejudices. Coyly using diminutives, he recounts how well-dressed little girls can shake coins out of gentlemen passers-by, how a schoolteacher addresses her richer pupils in a familiar way, how Jacinta's sister Benigna makes a good marriage – "a great household, fine fortune." Respectable and moderate in political views, this narrator likes money, well-cooked dishes and scrubbed little faces; he notes the difference between *decently dressed* students and riff-raff when Juanito is taken to the police station on St. Daniel's Eve, and protests at the outrageously florid style of a penniless Italian trumpet player when Guillermina and Father Nones prepare the last communion for Mauricia *la Dura*. Something about those musical flourishes *bites* into bourgeois sensibility. Similarly, the sight of the man's legs, gawking from too-short trousers, is almost an affront to him as well as to *la santa* – quick, says Guillermina to Jacinta, an old suit of Juan's to cover them up! Commenting on the outer façades of the convent, the narrator praises its clean, scrubbed look; cleanliness comes, of course, imported from France, and he abhors that plebeian tackiness of mixture and overlay he finds in both architectural style and music – the organ mixes vaudeville tunes and advertising jingles with the great church requiems. He shares the conservative self-righteousness of the Santa Cruz family, for it irks him to find that no one is in charge of making proper selection – permissiveness has corrupted Catholic rites.

Safety, smugness, status quo – in Part 1, Galdós's narrator manifests this social motif deeply embedded in Madrid's stratified, bourgeois culture. Everywhere the appearance of cloth is emphasized – in bedclothes, when on Christmas Day 1873 Juanito demands that sheets be arranged and pillows plumped. That "beveled" story-telling edge slips into view as Galdós places his narrator into this same group, endowing him "to some extent with the same preoccupations and prejudices, the same limited knowledge and the same liability to error as his fellows, while exempting the author *qua* author from identification with these views" (GR, 1977, 69).

Money and manners

In *Fortunata and Jacinta*, money, more than any other single factor, determines social class. Coming from mercantile districts in Old Madrid, the illustrious Santa Cruz family lives on Pontejos Square, named for the Marqués de Pontejos, who as mayor had renumbered city blocks and installed glinting lamp lights throughout the city; the name Pontejos stands for order, reform, enlightenment. At the same time, the family's cult of respectability and decency – cleanliness of the individual and social body – carries a residue of inquisitorial obsession with purity of blood, the name Santa Cruz suggesting that of converted Jews. Barbarita is a devout Catholic and at table no talk about other religions, even in jest, is tolerated. Protestantism, and particularly the Masonic order, are anathema, though Barbarita is less fanatic than Guillermina Pacheco, horrified at the pun *luto/luteranos* (mourning/Lutherans). This bit of "black" humor, *à propos* of the abject Nicanora who inks paper edges for funeral announcements, hints at a fanatical streak in *la santa*, a prominent member of the Santa Cruz circle. Unlike other great mercantile families in provincial cities of the North – bastions of feudal regionalism or of ultramontanism in support of don Carlos – no cleric joins family celebrations at the Santa Cruz house. Conservative Catholicism does not hold sway. But an ingrained, half-conscious anti-Semitism, expressed in the way people see the Jew as a racial type and as Christ-killer, does persist in Old Madrid, as indicated in Federico Ruiz's pronouncements on the Jewish origins of the Rubín family, the narrator's joking response, and the gutter speech of Izquierdo and Mauricia *la Dura*.

In Old Madrid, money – how it is made, what it buys – operates (the narrator now tells us) much as does a principle of physics, to determine family life and social class. Monetary equivalences are difficult if not impossible to assess when comparing mid-nineteenth-century Spanish society, whose middle class was just beginning to learn the art of spending, to today's entrenched, meritocratic and managerial professional class. In the Madrid of the 1840s and 1850s, the concept of "middle class" was in fact quite tenuous. Even as the narrator notes how that newly formed middle class stepped to center stage, exercising its energies in fullest measure, people like don Baldomero II did not feel secure, for they were tradesmen from humble beginnings, living in times of political and economic turmoil. Ever present was the fear of revolution, falling prices, and the pressing claims of an unruly, illiterate working class. Neither a university education nor professional training was available to more than a few, whereas the appearance of a cultivated manner was deemed essential to a person expected to rise in society. The narrator's ubiquitous use of military metaphors that allude to "social combat" discloses the unease and defensiveness that pervade the *placidez* of the Santa Cruz drawing room, as well as more modest households like Isabel Cordero's and doña Lupe's. Thus we witness the verbal sparring between the newly minted Marqués de Casa-Muñoz and Aparisi, a municipal deputy. Both men grope for *le mot juste*, mangling phrases in Italian, French and

Latin − "Un edificio *ad hoc*" opines Casa-Muñoz as Guillermina recounts the founding of her orphanage, and Aparisi
mistakes the meaning of that resonant remark of Galileo
"*eppur si muove*". Casa-Muñoz's pretentiousness, with his
false teeth and dyed sideburns, and Aparisi's foreign clichés
patched into speech betray working-class origins close at hand
− Izquierdo, a loud-mouthed street tough, recalls that don
Pascual Muñoz, father of the present Marqués, was a blacksmith and a hot-headed leader of a local revolutionary faction,
while Aparisi, rival to the Marqués in social refinement,
stockpiled lumber. As the narrator notes, for those who
lacked formal education it was imperative to cultivate a proper
appearance. As yet, there were no professional guilds to
protect tradesmen, nor educational requirements to keep
newcomers out.

Any comparison with the monetary value of currency in
present-day Spain is complicated further by the combined
influences of wages, inflation, national and international
economic and political circumstance. Spain in the 1870s was
essentially a pre-industrial society, now in rapid transition,
so that in the same family we find both old and new ways of
spending money. In Isabel Cordero's household, money goes
for food, not manufactured goods; she laments how quickly
heavy sacks of potatoes and vats of olive oil vanish − "pif"
− into thin air, whereas her sister-in-law Barbarita Santa
Cruz makes shopping her profession, buying on credit and
commissioning the best in meat, fish and wine. She can afford
to send out for chocolate, that staple of Spanish kitchens,
ordering it ground by a specialist in the trade, whereas thrifty
doña Lupe grinds chocolate herself at home. Shopping, for
Barbarita a consummate art, entails a social code that she
continually breaches in order to satisfy her *manía*. Privilege
calls for respect accorded to the lower classes, for the *art* of
shopping applies to luxury items, not necessities. But Barbarita
carries her obsession down to more visceral levels, corrupting
the commerce of the Plaza Mayor as stall keepers squabble
and fight for her favors. On those occasions, the narrator,
speaking of *doña Barbarita*, mixes *doña* with the diminutive,

a linguistic travesty that mixes the formal and familiar mode of address, allowing us to glimpse how a lady of high society, abusing privilege, elbows her way through the crowds. Luxury items are not native, and, except for enterprises like the great textile factories in Catalonia that Jacinta observes on her honeymoon, manufactured goods and packaged delicacies are imported – hardware, plum puddings and sauces from England, truffles and *champignons extra* from France, laces and silks from the Netherlands – Jacinta wears a raisin-colored *par-dessus* on her way to the tenement house of Mira el Río.

If, then, one takes standard currency equivalencies (four *reales* to the *peseta*, five *pesetas* to the *duro/peso*), multiplying these by ten, a rough estimate of comparative value and buying power between the *peseta* and today's American dollar may be established. Thus, all told, don Baldomero's fixed annual income of *25 mil pesos* amounts to some $1,250,000. He gives his son *mil duros* each semester, or $50,000. Barbarita receives from her husband a monthly allowance of *mil duretes*, again about $50,000, of which she gives Juanito another *dos o tres mil reales* each month, equivalent to $6,250. The *Delfín's* allowance each year from personal expenses thus comes to $175,000, truly a princely sum, especially when compared to the few pennies Nicanora earns by working all day edging mourning cards in black. Translating across times and cultures, one may compare the Santa Cruz family – regal, rich and politically well-connected – to the American Kennedys.

Money rules even more tenaciously in the lower middle class. It presides over doña Lupe's household, winking in the greasy gold of her late husband's portrait, in the usury of her partner Torquemada and in the ambitions of a host of office workers, clerics, professionals and small-time tradesmen – restless, aspiring people, prototypical of Larra's "*liquid man.*" Doña Lupe moves from the neighborhood of Salamanca to Chamberí and finally to Lavapiés. She marches off to auctions and flea markets, and surges to and fro in her thinking, out-pacing the narrator who must take "liquid measures" of a mind he compares to a storm-tossed sea. Juan Pablo rattles about the country as a traveling salesman, acts as a gunrunner for don Carlos, migrates from one café to another and molds his views to fit the Alfonsine regime as water fits the glass. Maxi's brother Nicolás pants after canonical rank and the usurer Torquemada makes money swell like "foam" or grow into "guano," his word for society's fertilizing agent.

Class consciousness is omnipresent. Strong-minded women, usually widows, head households (doña Lupe, doña Casta); emphasis is on family ties, education, getting ahead and imitating high society. Conversationalists in cafés divide into two categories: those with authority who sit on the sofas, backs to the wall, so as to preside as members of a tribunal, and those of lower rank who must pull up chairs. This "political" regime is breached, however, by don Basilio, ordinarily viewed as a commoner (*vulgo*), who foments a mini-revolt of the masses by taking his place on the sofa. Liberal views hold sway; masculine privilege is less entrenched, though always significant; self-interest motivates behavior and some opportunities for respectable employment do exist for women, like Aurora's position as floor manager in Pepe Samaniego's new boutique, financed by the banker don Manuel Moreno-Isla. In this fluid, unsettled "inner belt" of Spain's middle class, the money-making consciousness is sharper, less disguised than in the Santa Cruz drawing room, and this very frankness makes people less susceptible to snobbery. Doña Lupe's maternal nature and her managerial disposition, parallel to doña Bárbara's autocratic energies, are far more flexible, since doña Lupe admits a fallen women to the family and believes, though always with an eye to her own self-interest, in the possibility of moral reform. On the other hand, Jacinta cannot imagine what Juan's *mamá* would do if faced with a plebeian daughter-in-law who wore a shawl and cheap rings, who said "'*see ya later*' and couldn't even read." In both spheres, differences in social class stand more marked in the women, since for the most part only dress and deportment distinguish their efforts; women are not involved in politics, banking, or administrative work, although some do succeed in business, like Isabel Cordero, doña Lupe and doña Casta.

On the bottom step move indigents and poor people, sometimes employed, more often not − soldiers, wet nurses,
servants, prostitutes, beggars, gypsies, street urchins. Mira
el Río's tenement houses teem with desperate families like Ido
del Sagrario's. Only a few enjoy relative well-being (Severiana,
doña Fuensanta), and old-style patriarchal attitudes flourish
− even the child *Pituso* is "very much a male" and has,
Izquierdo boasts, "un talento macho." Yet even among the
poor, upward movement is discernible: at least Fortunata,
returning to la Cava, her place of origin, sees herself changed,
now quite respectable and certainly above the coarseness of
her aunt, gabbing and gesturing out in the open, bun a-bob.
While presented as a quintessential *madrileña*, a woman of
the people, Fortunata actually starts her story on the rise,
midway on the great stone stair. She appears shod in *botas*, a
factory-made, middle-class article, and one in which she takes
great pride. She lives in the center of Old Madrid, not in the
mudholes of Cuatro Caminos, origin of the little gypsy girl
Papitos, orphaned, destitute, without a single family relation.
Working as doña Lupe's servant girl, even *Papitos* moves up,
admiring Fortunata, frizzling her bangs to imitate the abundant
black curls of *la señorita*. Illiterate little *Papitos* and working-
class people of the slums make up what families like the Santa
Cruzes call the "fourth estate." In the end, however, what
such monied families do *not* see is how that "fourth estate"
of disenfranchised people intends to "square up" the social
pyramid, as shown by Mauricia *la Dura*'s rampage in Part 2.
The narrator's ironic use of equivalent terms for top and bottom
− the *reign* of don Baldomero II, the *empire* of the poor −
hints at exchange, and in effect, as Fortunata dies, the nether
world of la Cava becomes for a moment an "upper" room at
the top of the stair, far more sustaining in energies and values
than the great Santa Cruz house below.

Among social classes, certain groups of people move up
and down continuously on the steps of the great stone staircase.
Arnáiz's nephew, Gumersindo, does not have a commercial
bent, and it is his wife, Isabel Cordero, who saves the house
from ruin. Doña Casta starts out as a Moreno *rico* and ends

up a Moreno *pobre*. Eulalia Muñoz marries a *marqués*, rising in social status, while the narrator descends from the comforts of the Santa Cruz house to approach Fortunata, and perhaps, like Feijoo, falls in love with her. Movement finds balance in common preoccupations which lend coherence, a sense of "character," to a dense and diverse social body. High prices worry both Fortunata and Guillermina as they pick their way, arm in arm, along sidestreets; adultery is as much an obsession in the Santa Cruz house as in Maxi's mind, who finds a companion in misery in don José Ido del Sagrario.

Thus one class mimics the other, pointing to the ways historical and social contexts are worked out in a dialectic (1) as story-telling voices intersect; (2) as a few people move up and down the social staircase; (3) as political regimes (monarchy, republic) alternate, and (4) as the narrator, stretching and coiling the story line in panoramic views and intimate scenes, moves from partial reliability to a more instructed point of view, and from historiography to more varied discourse. Institutional details remain linked to character. Each consciousness inhabits concrete boundaries, sketching out a context either accepted, exploited, protested or transcended which becomes a part of a social system of interrelatedness (JPS, 108). The process requires "bifocals," so to speak: we must take alternating measurements, close-in and from afar, to assess this ambivalent social milieu, almost the way tailors cut and stitch in Old Madrid. On the one hand, the narrator presents the paradox of a society on the rise within a decadent regime; on the other, he shows how the persistence of local customs and older habits of mind determine a closely knit, yet relatively open, society, which at the same time harks back to primitive ways, remaining closed and impervious to change.

Old and New Madrid

The narrator's survey of the rise in fortune of the Santa Cruz Arnáiz family in Chapter 2, Part 1, argues for older ways. Although primitive and unwashed, people kept close to the family – doorways and storefronts, joined together, are alive with speech, close to the street; conversation goes cheek by jowl, as in the first sentence when the narrator inclines an ear to those bits of news from Villalonga, politician and gossiper. Houses connect so closely that one feels the breath of neighbors. People put a hand to the job and rely on the wisdom of popular sayings. But progress in industry, transport, finance, fashion and communication speeds things up, severing primal connections between buyer and seller, worker and product, parents and children. Thus as paper money and newly minted coins replace heavier *onzas*, as letters divide into paper and envelope, as credit becomes established and people, particularly women, buy on credit, something manipulative, even "phantasmagoric," slips in — now things are not what they seem. The notion of display effaces performance: in contrast to the style of old-fashioned storekeepers like Arnáiz or Estupiñá, Aurora Fenelón knows how to advertise fabric in the French way, enticing customers to buy. Publicity, Frenchified speech and sleights of hand have overtaken popular sayings and time-honored ways of doing things.

To the narrator, the manifest closeness of simpler ways — no waste, no inflation, no foreign cloth — is seen as fundamental to the good of society, in contrast to new tastes and technologies (advertisements, salesmen, envelopes, copiers) that divide wholes into parts, decoy the buyer and make debt a sign of social progress. Thus we can understand the shame of the decline of the exiled *mantón de Manila*, and the subtle, pernicious effects of Barbarita's shopping *manía* and her son's appetite for novelties. A strict upbringing had made don Baldomero something of a social "zagalote" — "countrified" and primitive like Old Madrid. When courting Barbarita, his conversation "rings like a cow bell" and his mouth comes "unstuck" like a ripe chestnut, prickling with ideas as sparse and spiny as his adolescent moustache. As a youth, Don Baldomero was stiff and formal, like a cigar-store Indian, but also hardworking, honest, affectionate and utterly faithful to Barbarita; their marriage is extolled as a model of reciprocity and respectability. Newer ways corrupt. Juanito is raised under the French sign of economic progress, and Arnáiz's misquotation "laisser aller, laisser passer" of the original phrase "Laisser faire, laisser passer" hints at the bungled upbringing of a boy who attends an elite, Frenchified grammar school and buys books at a French bookstore. Handsome, socially adept and clever in talk, the young "Dauphin," pretender to the throne of a commercial dynasty, will personify decadence in his idleness and caprice.

A look at politics, however, shows that older ways have perpetuated traditional abuses: monarchies and republics come and go, but the reign of the frock coat and finance remains the same, as does the political ethos − an opportunistic hodgepodge of opinions, which, as the narrator says, appear as patches on the cloth of those proverbial capes everyone wears. If political instability persists, so does the masculine prerogative, explicitly connected to politics, money and social class. Women think of themselves − and of men − as possessions, and in truth they have little else, receiving only the most rudimentary instruction and remaining confined to a narrow social role and to the kind of thinking that proposes, as a matter of course, two moral standards − one governing the conduct of men like Juanito Santa Cruz, another for "women and children." As that coarse priest Nicolás Rubín admonishes, women who forsake either marriage or a respectable spinsterhood face "the abyss," a patriarchal idea dramatized by the alcoholism of Mauricia *la Dura* or Segunda's dilapidated body. Not surprisingly, women themselves half-consciously use figures of speech and thought that equate male partners with money and ownership. The metaphors highlight the hostility in competitive relationships, as each woman sees the other as a "thief" or freebooting "pirate," and even, on occasion, physically assaults the other. In the marriage of old alligator-faced Quevedo, the notion of ownership, fueled by that Spanish obsession with honor, creates a pathological jealousy that deforms doña *Desdémona* into a circus fat lady.

All told, neither old ways nor the ways of progress portend enlightened change. Interconnecting *tertulias* in cafés suggest a collusion of political parties of every stripe, whereas the closeness of *tertulia* in Arnáiz's one-room store with its simple, staid, practical ethic is bound up with an incestuous closeness that inhibits new life in the Santa Cruz family. Everything corresponds and relates — story-telling splices social life together. " 'We're all one' " rejoices Arnáiz, not suspecting that he and don Baldomero, powerful, grown men, argue like children, their quarrels copied in the childish discussions of the young Santa heir, whose selfishness severs the very tie that Arnáiz celebrates with his universal claim. Within families, divisions blend; within the social body, barriers remain in place, even when breached.

But closeness also brings out the best in this tangled, story-telling world; closeness and the charm of institutions are allied (JPS, 108). The warmth of family life and the openness and ease of communication made Old and New Madrid, in the words of V.S. Pritchett, "a familiar place, entirely personal, without loneliness. It must be the only city without loneliness in the world." No one — except, perhaps, the wretched Villaamil — is left without support, in contrast to other social worlds depicted by Balzac, Dickens, Flaubert. Family loyalty is immediate, effective — doña Lupe snatches up her shawl to have a talk with the teacher when things go badly for Maximiliano, and marshals every resource to help Juan Pablo in jail. In the midst of seaminess and squalor, Ido's little family gathers round the table for a joyful supper, thanks to *la santa's* provisions. Although Moreno-Isla, exiled and uprooted, dies alone in his room, Guillermina stands on tip-toe outside the door.

Tertulias offer more than diversion or political favoritism — solace in grief, friendship in loneliness, job opportunities and, on occasion, instruction of the highest order. Café tables connect people as do branches of the great family tree, providing a forum for Juan Pablo, a home for street people like Refugio and shady ladies like doña Nieves. Both women preside over gatherings in cafés as Barbarita entertains guests in her drawing room. Everyone is at ease with the human body — the lofty Marqués de Muñoz opines on Juanito's runny nose as if the Marqués were a nursemaid or a *mamá*; everyone uses a down-to-earth, native (*castizo*) speech. People are generous in spontaneous ways − after cutting Estupiñá in on the winning lottery ticket, don Baldomero buys an accordion for the counterfeit child, *el Pitusín*.

We also recall how naturally the middle-class Rubín family accepts Fortunata, a woman of the streets. Here is a situation hardly imaginable in any other nineteenth-century European novel. Once "purified" in the convent, Fortunata can take her place next to doña Lupe almost as an equal; they cook the wedding dinner together. Friends come to the wedding and doña Silvia, Torquemada's wife, arrives wearing the great Manila shawl. She consciously mixes *pueblo* and middle class to surround the bride with a new social context, and even doña Lupe, miffed, must hold her tongue. People find it as natural as breathing that Fortunata lives with doña Lupe, sews at the window, thrashes things out, joins *tertulias*, meets her friends − in short, that she is adopted (MN, 194). Adults show effusive affection to children; men embrace each other and the formal and familiar modes of address mix in relationships. Galdós depicts every register of maternal feeling − Jacinta's obsession, Barbarita's veneration, doña Lupe's "tough love" for Maxi, and Guillermina's intrusive wish to adopt Fortunata's child. The narrator's warm, equable tone pays respect to every living thing, as he takes note of people like the little hump-backed newspaper woman and her brother, who move among café tables, flailing right and left with copies of *La Correspondencia*. Novels and newspapers correspond, thus maintaining a familiar mix of energies in Old and New Madrid.

Arnáiz's words about all as one not only connect the closeness of family life with social class, but also point to the reciprocity of institutions, living speech, and contemporary novels like *Fortunata and Jacinta*. It is neither the golden age nor utter decadence but a combination, as Ballester says, of "raw" and "cooked" fruit. The brute rawness of *pueblo*, mixed with the confections of an industrialized culture, find a correlative in his theory of mixed styles, so appropriate to realist fiction, which he and Ponce formulate as they ride back from Fortunata's funeral. They reflect on the story of her life, imagining that story as a mixed genre — a "play or novel" — and recognize that while a novel should mirror life the way it is, the substantive facts of "raw fruit" need to be spiced by art in the manner of a "compote" if one is to express the whole of what is real. Thus by associating the life story of a former illiterate working-class girl who learns to tell her own story with a self-conscious, distinctly literary idea about what a novel is, this homely pharmacist suggests how the very notion of a novel within a novel and of life as art function as parts intrinsic to social change, to the phenomenon of a rising social status personified not only by Fortunata but also manifest in almost every neighborhood of Old Madrid.

In effect, art and upward social mobility do appear to *relate* on more than one level, causing us to observe certain similarities between *pueblo* and high bourgeoisie. In Part 1, Juanito had mocked the coarseness of Fortunata's uncle, the plebeian Izquierdo, nicknamed *Platón* for the way he gobbled huge plates of vegetable stew. But by Part 4, *Platón* (Plato) has moved up in the world — now he gobbles the fruits of that leafy family tree, earning a place on Pontejos Square as the uncle of the child Jacinta adopts. Once again, the family tree has become a self-conscious figure of speech. It is something explicitly artistic that works, says the narrator, because its branching connections reveal how the *pueblo* now hobnobs with idle, middle-class *señoritos*. What works, of course, is quite ironic: Izquierdo, drunk, lazy and loud-mouthed, "works" as an artist's model, posing like Santa Cruz before history's mirror, while Juanito "works" by simply posing as a man of many obligations. Both men turn into images of a specific, literary kind: Santa Cruz sees himself in that mirror as a conqueror, seeking either to deflower working-class girls or regain his wife's favors, and Izquierdo poses as Hernán Cortés or Nebuchadnezzar. Both men, *pueblo* and *señorito*, represent social extremes that overlap, and both men, in their self-conscious way of copying, reflect the social pretensions of the times.

Closeness here is neither compact nor dense, as in Clarín's *La Regenta*. It is permeable — everything branches out and breathes, everything connects and corresponds and in the end, the old *costumbrista* packsaddle and mule harness has been raised to noble Babieca's reins: we glimpse the figure of El Cid's great horse in Ballester's concluding point about how good and bad, once "yoked together" in harness, "go walking around." Thus this steady, good man suggests that redemption is still possible if one accepts compromise, the mix of one thing with another − this is, after all, his particular recipe for realism in art, which combines "raw fruit" − the bare physical facts − with a cooked, seasoned "compote," meaning the emotional and spiritual effect of those facts on human consciousness. This spells out the achieved realism of Galdós's own novel, which also artfully combines the two stories of Fortunata and Jacinta.

Chapter 2

Characters and configurations

Two-by-fours

The entrepreneurial energies of the age appear to build character as Galdós assembles the novel in four parts and juxtaposes titles and subtitles to reflect a dialectic within the patriarchal consciousness that dominates the times. The names of the two protagonists, unattached to married surnames, show how Fortunata and Jacinta preside over the novel, whereas the four parts correspond to the introduction of four male characters, whose presence initially places the two women in the background. Once the story starts, however, imagistic progressions create a female mode as the bird-egg motif mounts up, culminating in the birth of the child. The two main organizing principles — four (male) divisions and the bird-egg motif (female) — which build the unity of the four parts, converge in the child who resolves the dialectic by reconciling the two women.

As the two stories develop within four parts, building with two-by-fours becomes a unifying motif, since the characters as well as the author act as builders. In the role of social historian, the narrator builds his account of the Santa Cruzes with the wood and running vines of the family tree. Guillermina founds her orphanage, petitioning stone, bricks, beams. Barbarita stockpiles provisions as barricades go up in the streets, and holds forth on architecture in her drawing room. In the Rubín household, doña Lupe builds up capital while Nicolás builds his ecclesiastical career on the edification of Fortunata, "digging a foundation" upon which Feijoo will reconstruct and restore the broken Rubín marriage. Fortunata enters Las Micaelas as the convent is being built, outer walls rising, brick by brick, to block her from Maxi's view. Moreno-Isla finances the boutique that Pepe Samaniego builds for his cousin Aurora, while Ballester mixes a mustard plaster,

building good will, building toward his own twinned representation of Fortunata's life, conceived as a "play or a novel"
as he talks to a friend.

The concrete structural analogies that build the dialectical
realism of *Fortunata and Jacinta* originate in dialogue; the
first sentence, spoken in ordinary, conversational Spanish,
establishes the interrelatedness that shapes and develops
character. Talkative Estupiñá, a fixed presence at beginning
and end, provides, in Gilman's words, "a flat oral frame for
a three-dimensional oral world" (SG, 267). This notion of a
"flat oral frame" specifies an important link between speech,
character and configuration in *Fortunata and Jacinta*. On
the one hand, live speech determines action and scene. As
Villalonga, the novel's arch con-*spira*-tor, breathes those first
bits of news, the novel appears to be talking to itself, with
the arranging hand of an author scarcely visible, for the
opening sentence presents a narrator who listens, gestures
and speaks, passing on information with a wave of the hand:
"The earliest news I have about the person who bears this
name [Juanito Santa Cruz] comes from my friend Jacinto
María Villalonga, and goes back to the time when he and
other friends – this one here, that one over there – Zalamero,
Joaquinito Pez, Alejandro Miquis – went about the lecture
halls at the University." ("Las noticias más remotas que tengo
de la person que lleva este nombre me las ha dado Jacinto
María Villalonga, y alcanzan al tiempo en que este amigo
mío y el otro y el de más allá, Zalamero, Joaquinito Pez,
Alejandro Miquis, iban a las aulas de la Universidad" 97.)
On the other hand, those same bits of news recall a chapter
title ("Juanito Santa Cruz"), signaling how characterization
will evolve through a specifically literary structure: a titled
name at the beginning, juxtaposed to a concluding title that
flatly states the end ("Final"), transmits an unspoken fact
about Juanito Santa Cruz: he does not count for much in
the new novel that Jacinta imagines. The juxtaposition appears
to sum up his story rather ironically, because as he disappears
from the text at the end we know who he really is.

This combination of speech and sign works at every level of

characterization in *Fortunata and Jacinta*. Speech defines character, and, once transcribed into patterns, causes character to develop as people react verbally to one another, particularly to improvised or unfamiliar situations: Guillermina, inhibited by the thought of Jacinta eavesdropping in the next room, cannot find the right words. Flustered, guilty, her style changes, and she spouts a few hackneyed phrases of condemnation to Fortunata (SG, 267). This speech "act" or "encounter" shows that *la santa* is not quite what she seems. And as Galdós experiments with new forms of inward, subvocal thinking and inarticulate sounds, the concept of character extends beyond linguistic and social norms. Styles of speech, alternating with silences, correspond, then, to the first term of Galdós's equation for realism, whereas structure and analogy associate character with new designs. As Rodgers observes, this changing, dual perspective permits a deflationary irony that allows us to perceive all shades and gradations along the whole spectrum of attitudes and behaviors, including pretentiousness or *donjuanismo*, self-dramatization and self-deception (ER, 1978, 28). Thus "there are grounds for saying that Galdós is less concerned with imitating the flux of life than with enabling us, as it were, to see behind the surface of this life to the principles that determine it, and to form judgements about the value or otherwise of these principles" (ER, 1978, 70).

The evolution of character through configuration appears on the page as a developing event. Spoken words, passed through recurring patterns, turn into animated things that "seem to fly as spontaneously as birds from a speaker here to a listener there, alive in their biographies and in their shared histories" (SG, 258). It is a living, spoken word, lodged in memory and felt to be as tangibly real as any body or bit of material and to display a native "character," to recall Moreno-Isla's thought as he hears the song of a gypsy street urchin. To mark this enlarged concept of living speech, memory and image, reifying word and sign as "bodies," Galdós conceives character and configuration as one. He builds new dimensions within commonplace speech and ordinary people so that even things as stupidly plain as a plate of beans, which the priest

Nicolás compares to the probable outcome of Fortunata's adultery, have their story to tell.

Pyramids, triangles, pairs

In Old Madrid a hierarchical pyramid specifies triangles among lovers and spouses, as marriages produce inversions of roles and as the relationships of women to each other and to male family members undergo change. On top − *primero y derecho* − we find the Santa Cruzes, conservative, rich, powerful; on the bottom − *segundo e izquierdo* − frantically leftist, second-rate scramblers like Fortunata's aunt Segunda Izquierdo; in the middle, households like doña Lupe's, doggedly maintaining a toe-hold on the social ladder. The Santa Cruz pyramid sits upon that straight Trujillo line. While French notions of economic progress influence Juanito's upbringing, ideas about the practical advantages of marriage derive from Spanish packsaddles and mule harnesses. The narrator, always an entrepreneur of language, recounts the history of family ties in muleteer speech. The Trujillo *mamás*, descendants of that Extremeñan harness maker, trace a short, straight line in their thinking from idea to action. One tugs at the reins to get her way while the other pushes plans into line to marry off Baldomero and Barbarita.

The narrator's metaphor of harnessed mules, used to describe the arrangement of both Santa Cruz marriages, hints at the paradox of progress and regress. Marriages flourish as the family tree unfurls, but at the same time everything keeps contracting to that frowning Trujillo "bar of steel." Elder and junior Santa Cruzes appear to prosper as a family, yet they remain yoked together under one roof, "more like two couples" than a family, for Barbarita has transformed Jacinta into a kind of leash (*calza*) that ties her son to her maternal rule in the manner of a muleteer. Each Santa Cruz couple marries in May, their union either "cooked-up" ("amasado y cocido") or "crafted" in the manner of a business venture ("la empresa aquella de la calza"), and names present a similar linguistic pattern: both parents' names start with B

(Baldomero, Barbarita), both children's with J (Juanito, Jacinta), each pair displaying the same structure of accented vowels. A tight phonetic symmetry draws up that leash, while the diminutives of mother and son (Barbarita, Juanito) cross couples, intimating split pairs and perfidious new love triangles, at cross-purposes to marriage. The founding, matriarchal Trujillo harness leaves no space, no breath, for the desired Santa Cruz heir (AG, xix). Thus Juan and Jacinta's marriage, arranged to strengthen the family, stands the pyramid of power on its head. Whereas the father made money, the idle son spends it, managing "by dint of clever financing" to spend it in ways that convince the unwary household that he is *not* spending it. Half-truths, a keen commercial sense and infantile appetites are facts of character that invert the social pyramid, placing the Santa Cruz heir on the bottom, and the scrofulous Ido, clutching a coin to his shirt, on top.

In his initial characterization of the Santa Cruz family Galdós threads motifs (family tree, cloth, money) through geometric figures (pyramids, pairs, straight lines). His aim, in part, is to reveal "character" as façade and to manipulate changing triangular figures to show that power, inhering in appearances only, is a danger to the social body. The character-ization of Juanito evolves through visual analogies that reveal in his superficial and banal character a serious and invisible, unrecognized social problem. To flag this point in Part 1, the narrator takes care to "dress up" his own fabricated image: Madrid's social body is portrayed as a "huge pyramid at whose peak sits the top hat." Now the family tree has become a "clothes" tree and perched on top is Juanito Santa Cruz, "dressed up in intellectual airs, in a frock coat cut from ready-made ideas with the lapels of language pressed flat."

The characterization of Jacinta differs markedly from that of her husband. Whereas the economics of family ties confer power on him, they abort power in her. As one of Arnáiz's seven daughters, Jacinta forms part of the burden that un-married women present to heads of households. To marry off daughters is to place them advantageously – "*colocar* bien las siete chicas" advises the narrator. Here the verb meaning "to place" also refers to the act of investing a sum of money, and the absence in the phrase of what is termed the "personal *a*" always used in Spanish to distinguish people from things, signals that daughters are not "people" but goods and chattels. This patriarchal attitude is developed further by the narrator's use of mercantile figures of speech and the imagery of domestic animals in descriptions of Jacinta's mother Isabel Cordero and her brood.

In effect, Isabel Cordero, always "a martyr to duty," intends to sell her daughter into marriage and her sister-in-law doña Bárbara, the consummate shopper, is a ready buyer, alert to the "treasures" of her niece's loving heart that "pays back with interest" the smallest sign of affection. In the manner of a Trujillo *mamá*, Bárbara plots the marriage, designing the role of wife, cutting a "calza" and making her little Cinderella fit the shoe. Jacinta is brought (bought) into the family "to tie up a chicken," or again to break in a kicking mule; she will serve as a hobble upon the wayward son, ironically and to her great grief reinforcing maternal ties. No thought is given to Juanito's need for self-discipline, as he continues to think and act according to his mother's will, ruling, as does a child, through her small tyrannies. Marriage does raise Jacinta to royalty: as *la Delfina*, she will reign over Madrid. Her name "Hyacinth" means "born to the purple," the blue and red of the flower evoking also the traditional colors of the Virgin's robes (AG, 1986, xx). Privilege notwithstanding, however, Jacinta's position at the peak of the pyramid cloaks a betrayal. In Part 1, family ties, unraveled prodigiously, obscure the sketch of her face and figure. Social connections appear to be what is important; they come first and deflect perceptions of Jacinta's character – her light step and expressive gestures. Even her marriage, chief event of her life and of the novel's plot, is at first briskly set aside as the narrator, busy with other threads, snips off his story. The snip treats Jacinta as simply a product of social circumstance – *la Delfina* is a person strictly conditioned to serve certain ends. Here, then, is a small, modest leaf, quickening amid the foliage of the great family tree.

Partners on the stair

The narrator turns from Jacinta's snipped-off story to that "trifling page" which is what he terms Juanito's *novela*. On a visit to Estupiñá the boy descends from the house on Pontejos Square to la Cava de San Miguel, the most primitive, deepest enclosure of Old Madrid. A door beckons. Juanito steps into a poultry shop and tries to stay clear of the mess, but boots crush egg shells, blood-splotched feathers stick, beaks peck a pantleg; bodies of chickens dangle wretchedly and jerk toward a slaughterer who grabs, throttles and throws each shuddering corpse to the pluckers. All attests to "man's limitless voracity," says the narrator, associating destructive appetites with the Santa Cruz heir. Through an entry way a stone stair rises, half castle, half prison; a door stands ajar, in between floors ("entresuelo"). Santa Cruz hesitates, turns, takes a look and sees ... a woman − young, pretty, quick in movement. Catching sight of a stranger, she "ruffles her feathers," stepping, arching, arms akimbo, shawl and skirts filling, aswirl with movement − pointed toe, high heel, mittened hands ... a raw egg. They speak, she offers him the remains of the egg; jellied, transparent whites ooze through her fingers. Juanito refuses: raw eggs repel him. She takes a step, lifts the broken egg to her lips, sucks the yolk, drops the shell. We hear the cry "¡*Fortunaaá*¡", her screeched reply, the sound of skirts slapping on the stair. Then all is silent.

A dramatic glimpse, a snipped-off story: these two ways of presenting Fortunata and Jacinta sketch a basic similarity while emphasizing differences. The narrator gives two thumb-nail portraits, each articulating a self-contained space. Features are dabbed in brush-strokes that accentuate movement − Fortunata's ruffled feathers, Jacinta's darting gestures. Both women display artistic temperaments: *la Delfina* epitomizes elegance in dress and manner while Fortunata steps forward elegantly shod, and in the scene, shawl, scarf, skirt and mittened hand are harmoniously disposed. Both views are partial, brief, since each woman, in differing ways, stands eclipsed by considerations of money, commerce and social class. Family history disqualifies Jacinta, but doña Bárbara works from within to cultivate that *calza* in her prospective daughter-in-law. Fortunata first appears as a social type, not an individual person. Both portraits also recall a fairy-tale plot: on Pontejos Square, Jacinta is Cinderella, her godmother/stepmother is doña Bárbara, her prince is *el Delfín*. In la Cava, Fortunata standing on the great stone stair ("half castle, half prison") is a Sleeping Beauty who waits for her prince. He arrives in blood-splattered boots.

The glimpses pair the character and plight of each woman, while obvious differences start the tension between them. Jacinta peeps out from the social text; she is a story that stays put, *shoed* into the house, whereas Fortunata emerges as *conceived* in la Cava; she is born from an egg, *shod* for streetlife, and she takes a first step in a *novela* that a prince carries about him. We sense an intake of air as the narrator pauses, then an exhalation as feathers fluff; there is a refreshing sense of freedom in the stepped-up sexuality of those *botas* – pointed toe, bright heel. Not for Juan the thrift of saving steps by entering through Dámaso Trujillo's shoe store "The Lily Branch" – no more branching family relations, no more *shoes, please* – his first thought is only for those leather boots. Formal, linear depiction sets Jacinta upon a *pouff* in her parlor, in line with doña Bárbara's point of view. A tumultuous rendering of Fortunata builds on bird and egg motifs, metonymic images that depict accumulation in pieces and parts. It is not a total view, requiring distance, but a foreshortened impact as images work beneath the consciousness of both character and narrator to structure the episode internally. Fortunata fills space; space swells, rounded like an egg; space empties as abrupt silence seems to suck the "yolk." Santa Cruz craves that yolk, craves all the rounded rawness of la Cava.

In retrospect, the encounter appears as an emblematic moment. It plots action, establishes character and symbolizes, as would an emblem, the beginning and end of a story that starts up *in medias res*: Fortunata emerges through a doorway, in-between floors, midway on a stair. She steps from the chicken shop (naturalist subject) toward her "slaughterer," aspiring in love but submissive to a boot heel stuck with crushed shells and feathers. Blood-splattered feathers presage her eventual death in blood-spotted sheets. This impressionistic technique, sketched within a balanced composition, recalls Velázquez, cited in Galdós's early essay of 1870 as a precursor of a distinctively Spanish realism. We glimpse the great painting of *Las meninas* as, like Velázquez, the narrator appears to work at the easel while Juan enters and Fortunata exits, up or down the stair.

Puntos negros

Rich in painterly detail as this scene is, what is left out is significant as well, for Fortunata's anonymity, her half-articulated name and ensuing silence suggest a life not quite signified, something hushed and about to begin. Again, like Velázquez's impressionistic juxtapositions of light and color, Galdós's technique is pointillistic: dot-like images conjure up a tumultuous presence as Fortunata emerges from spaces between points. Throughout Part 1 Galdós develops her characterization through this configuration of "dots" (*puntos*) – brief, sketchy views. For example, once Juanito returns from la Cava, the narrator defers to doña Bárbara who screws up her eyes to catch a glimpse of the affair. Fortunata starts to surface as she influences Juan's speech and dress – low-life torero talk, pegged pants and rakish gestures. Barbarita sends Estupiñá to spy; more bits and pieces emerge, tattled from a distance – Juan and Villalonga, a supper at Sobrino Botín's, two lower-class women described as "a pair of stampeding heifers." Abruptly, gossip ceases. Even parroting old don Plácido refuses to talk. Something's up. Ruffians bang at the door, Juan evades contact and Barbarita knows her "lost" boy is saved, while the narrator's use of the word "salvamento" suggests the irony of something "salvaged," like junk metal. But Barbarita only sees in that "unknown page" an amorous escapade or two – a necessary stage, a childish disease, like measles – and she sets out to secure his future by embarking upon the business venture of that "calza."

Indirect, intermittent views of Fortunata persist to the
close of Part 1, refracted through the viewpoint of the Santa
Cruz family. On the honeymoon, Juan's evasive replies shrink
Barbarita's "trifling page" to a "parenthesis," as he says.
But soon the "parenthesis" cracks open like that raw egg
on the stair, spilling turbulent images as Jacinta pries details
from her reluctant husband, dreams of the episode and engages
in involuntary, associative thinking. Little, stabbing dots —
the sight of red cloth, a vendor's cry, working girls in factories,
a light snuffed out — these cluster in her consciousness as
"black dots" (*puntos negros*). She herself invents the image.
The "black dots" trace out her perception of an underlying
centrifugal force that ruins the honeymoon, blights the marriage
and alters her own way of thinking. Outside the train window,
birds perch on telegraph wires, and in a station Juan buys
his bride a special treat — succulent, fried birds, "a mound
of little corpses." The image, picked out in italics, links birds-
in-the-background, chicken-victims and a bird-child, and
dot-like birds sketch out Fortunata's presence on the honeymoon (AG, 1974, 57). That night, Jacinta presses her husband
for a name. The name arises as it steps down the page in
dialogue. It is articulated, in hesitations, between husband
and wife, finally to be spoken by Jacinta. The dot-like, stepped
syllables suggest how Jacinta and Fortunata, on the honeymoon, have become, for a moment, partners on the stair:

— Se llama *For...*	Her name is *For...*
— *For...narina.*	*For...narina.*
— No. *For...tuna...*	No. *For...tuna...*
— *Fortunata.*	*Fortunata.*

In Sevilla, after a bout of drinking, Juan trots Jacinta on
his knees. Restlessness, confession: here, a pained sense of
duty toward his bride; there, clustered in darkness, Fortunata
— starry eyed, doves at breast, mother-dove, all as one.
Idealized, dot-like images alternate with glimpses of an illiterate
gypsy girl, dirty and dishonored, her hands coarsened by hard
work. Between two dots, we see a wrong done, which Jacinta
resolutely acknowledges as she lights a small lamp in her heart

for her rival. Another wrong is done by naming: love on the honeymoon comes used off the rack, like second-hand clothing. Terms of endearment (*nena, paloma*) already belong to Fortunata, the named one, born (*nata*) of chance or fortune (*fortuna*). Duty, not love, ties Juan to his wife; childish play, not passion, characterizes their intimacy. Now a final, ironic *punto*: a wedding trip, taken by train, turns out to stay stuck on the great stone stair. Already Jacinta lives in one context while she senses herself suddenly destined for another. The connections between *puntos negros* show how she chafes between an old self and a strange, involuntary, new way of thinking.

Back in Madrid and settled at home, those two dot-images of Fortunata — idealized beauty, beaten-down slave — alternate as bits of news disturb the decorum of the Santa Cruz house. Two years after the honeymoon the starving hack writer, don José Ido del Sagrario, presents himself at the door. He has serial magazines to sell, also his own *novela* about the abandoned child *et Pituso*, supposedly Fortunata's son by Juanito. Ido whispers his melodramatic version about a brazenly good-looking tart who abandons her child — that "little egg dealer" (*hueverito*) whom Jacinta had imagined on the honeymoon. To prove *Pituso* counterfeit, Juan comes up with a quick sketch of a battered Fortunata, trailing after the coffin of their infant son. At the close of Part 1, this dot-image contrasts stunningly with Villalonga's gossipy report of having seen Fortunata in a café, transformed into a splendid Parisian mistress. But, after another turn of fortune, she is back on the streets in working-class clothes. Both images incite Juan's imagination and he starts up another *novela*, a fiction that is French in origin. Now Villalonga's dot-images collapse the living lung as pneumonia strikes and the *res*, the animal *thing*, slips away.

In Part 1, the dot-images used to characterize Fortunata draw a figure that expresses the social situation of her story. The figure consists of a seris of black dots (*puntos negros*) that appear intermittently, pressing against social norms which may be visualized as that straight Trujillo line. A curious triangle results: on top, social codes, marital alignments and linear descriptions draw straight lines which peak to become the social pyramid. From below, a surging curve of black dots intersects the line of decorum that represents the base of the triangle. The curve sketches out Fortunata's subliminal presence in Jacinta's mind as a *punto negro*, an obsessive presence that disrupts the honeymoon and penetrates the household. In this way, Fortunata forms the love triangle without appearing to be a discernible part of the social pyramid.

This dual configuration characterizes one woman in terms of the other. Part 1 is told from the vantage point of the Santa Cruz family: narration highlights Jacinta and suppresses Fortunata except for the encounter on the stair. Part 2 focuses on Fortunata, while Jacinta is glimpsed from behind church railings or becomes a dot-image in Santa Cruz's conversations with Fortunata. Part 3 centers upon both women and depicts their confrontation outside Mauricia *la Dura*'s bedroom and in Guillermina's house. Now each protagonist becomes a *punto negro* for the other: on the balcony, as King Alfonso enters Madrid, Jacinta receives a "pistol shot" of news as Juan renews the affair. In the account, whispered to her by a treacherous friend, Fortunata appears as a raven-haired femme fatale, a "black dot" that incites Jacinta to confront her husband. In the tenement house of Mira el Río, Mauricia *la Dura* presents Fortunata with two polar images of her rival, one as "la Jacinta" – a "goody two-shoes," a "thieving monkey" – and another simply as "Jacinta," using the name without the definite article to show her as angelic, a "seraphim." Part 4 concentrates on Fortunata, with some partial views of Jacinta, who imagines one last dot-image of her rival, the embrace that reconciles the two women.

Triads on Pontejos Square

The Santa Cruz marriage forms the classic love triangle – wife, husband, lover. This triangle, persisting throughout, keeps forming and reforming, always a variation on the same pattern, with Fortunata as the fixed angle; she is the only character who breathes the atmosphere of all three social classes. Triangular relationships change between women as well as between women and men – parenthood also is presented in a triangle, as shown in the child's three names of Juan Evaristo Segismundo, in Fortunata's idea of *tres mamás* and in the family Jacinta imagines, consisting of herself, the newborn child and Moreno-Isla (AG, 1974, 52).

Juanito and Jacinta's marriage divides the Santa Cruz family into a double unit: two couples, two bedrooms, two marital relationships. Society's pyramid defines this dual structure of changing pairs. Men and money rule: the patriarchal don Baldomero doles out monthly sums; Juan, adored as a fairy-tale prince, reigns supreme; male guests find Guillermina's story a joke and pass to the drawing room "to talk about serious matters like business or politics." But men rule only through powerful matriarchal figures; they abdicate responsibility while retaining power. Just as doña Isabel's energetic resolve and financial acumen had led her to eclipse her husband, good old Gumersindo, so doña Bárbara runs the household, sets the pace, spends the money, rears the child, arranges his marriage, and manages that marriage thereafter. In Part 1, her point of view controls narrative perspective, for in differing ways both Jacinta and Fortunata appear diminished by her pre-eminence in the story. Toward the end, this powerful matron recedes from view but her prestige remains intact, if not increased, for we note that it is "señora doña Bárbara," not Jacinta or Juan, who figures most prominently in Fortunata's thoughts at the birth of her son, "to the manor born."

In this way, the outer, conventional triad – Baldomero–Barbarita–Juanito – reverses within the family to stand as Barbarita–Juanito–Baldomero. Similarly, the triad Juanito–Barbarita–Jacinta tips over to become Barbarita–Juanito–Jacinta. These inversions of role modify the triads still further, resulting in an unspoken collusion between mother and son. Barbarita buttresses the male at the top while consigning her daughter-in-law to the bottom. She assumes a submissive, worshipful role while exercising authority in the son's name. Jacinta finds herself caught in a double bind, betrayed by her own sex and blood relation. Coerced subservience to doña Bárbara pays off handsomely for the only son and heir who rules effortlessly and without restraint. As a "subjugated" wife Jacinta must bow beneath that old Trujillo yoke, although, like her mother-in-law, she idolizes Juanito and adapts quickly to the role of surrogate mother.

Thus the junior Santa Cruz marriage, founded upon a shared adoration, is a failure from the start. Chief among the reasons is the way Barbarita usurps the role of the wife. The process takes place beneath the decorum of family life, surfacing in the related motifs of cloth, thread and ties, episodes like the arrangement of the marriage, the honeymoon and ensuing conjugal relationships. The process, not unlike the configuration of "black dots" that perforated scenes on the honeymoon, suggests a familiar axis of mother/lover, as doña Bárbara keeps bursting into the bedroom. She inverts the roles of wife—mother by depersonalizing Jacinta, even as she reifies her daughter-in-law as a serviceable tool (*calza*). Now as a wife Jacinta must be, above all, motherly, a nurturing *mujer-madre*, in short, a reflection or duplication of Barbarita herself. Significantly enough, Barbarita bears quite a resemblance to Jacinta. She is slender, elegant, as youthful-looking as her daughter-in-law, really pretty, just a darling ("monísima") – precisely the adjective the narrator will apply to the young bride – and in Part 1 the narrator often refers to her with the diminutive. Other parallels reinforce the similarity between the two women: their arranged marriages, desire for children and fear of sterility. Their kinship to one another as aunt and niece, doubled again as mother and daughter-in-law, equates and reverses the identities of wife and mother. The stage is set for the jealous mother to take Jacinta's place, to neutralize and corrupt the wifely role so that there will be no competition for the son's affections.

In this way the marriage incestuously binds mother to son. We perceive in Barbarita's playful but firm admonishments to Juanito the seeds of a sterile union; no marriage so vitiated at the root can ever prosper and grow. Another incestuous tie constricts the marriage since Juan and Jacinta, first cousins and reared from childhood in the same house, are more like brother and sister. They are almost the same age, have slept in the same bed, quarreled over the same toys and received equal punishments from the same mother. Little sexuality can exist between two people who treat each other "with brotherly affection." How, Juan wonders, can two cradles become a marriage bed? The transition is made "like silk," that slippery, silken touch even now associated with betrayal. The marriage starts off in separate beds, canopied in blue silk, the cold, outer trappings of luxury having supplanted any closeness. Jacinta wears a blue silk gown in an important dream that shows how she has been cheated of motherhood, and Santa Cruz, who insists Fortunata pose as a "feline" Parisian prostitute, berates her for not wearing a silk dressing gown. Silk, here a symbol of deception, points to another incestuous tie as Jacinta, sister to Juan, becomes his mother, and fertility and sterility become two sides of the coin that has bought and bound her to the family.

Cloth, coins and a "calza" that hobbles make an untenable marriage contract. Santa Cruz's sexuality, shunted into the low-life of Old Madrid, becomes neutralized at home through rituals of childish play. On the honeymoon, Juanito teaches his wife to cosset and spoil, to say "chí" in a baby way, to flirt and fool innocently – kisses are "stolen," he wants to be cradled, signs of adult affection are frankly asexual. Whenever Juan is propelled toward Jacinta by the pushes and pulls of appetite, childishness and maternal *mimo* result – grimaces, spanks, tickles and hide-and-seek games. He revels in unabashed infantile regressions, crying for the teat in intimate moments, playing upon his wife's maternal nature. Respect for their social position always prevails, however, since both elder and junior Santa Cruzes fear scandal and Juan seeks periodically to "taste" his wife's purity, preening before the polished glass of her virtue. However, any feeling of respect he may have for her, scarcely acknowledged in any event, always has that competitive edge as between siblings.

So the good times are flawed and brief enough. Married only two years, Juan has been unfaithful at least five or six times, an average of an affair every four months. Rarely does Jacinta regain her husband's affection; intimacy is contrived, a favor to be earned in exchange for her most private thoughts. Excepting playful moments, Juan ensures that indifference and decorum rule. Given the emotional incest of the union, spontaneous adult intimacy is taboo. When liquor loosens his tongue on the honeymoon, he blurts out the truth of his passion for Fortunata and his sense of duty toward his wife. Settled at home, he pronounces upon the platonic character of their relations, making speeches about proper marital roles and the "reasonableness" of turtledoves. Their separate beds stand in contrast to the double bed of the parents, a huge, rambling structure with ornate columns and a helmeted bedstead. The elder couple sit together at the theater. Jacinta and Juan occupy separate seats, she lower down, he higher up, with a clique of male friends.

Who is sterile?

The Oedipal nature of the marriage raises a question about Jacinta's inability to conceive. Sterility appears as a physical impairment, a kind of retribution for possession of money and privilege. Jacinta does not bear Juanito a child; Fortunata does. But Fortunata lives her life far removed from doña Bárbara's damaging rule. The son can periodically recover his manhood with this orphaned woman of the people, so sexual and uninhibited. No threat of incest stifles their relationship, though it is grossly exploitative in other ways. The changing triangles and pairs, however, point to barrenness as the result of larger deficiencies and usurpations of role. With respect to his wife, as in García Lorca's play, Juan is *yermo* (barren) within an inbred bourgeois household. In that household, Jacinta has no place, no function, no identity of her own, since Fortunata, as Juan's mistress, has supplanted her as a conjugal partner. In order to treat his wife with even a modicum of courtesy, Juan must confect in his mind's eye the image of a courtesan gowned in silk. Even at times when the pendulum swings toward home, affection and money go hand in hand — his effusive grip wrinkles the paper bills he gives his wife in a rare moment of indulgence.

Doña Bárbara takes over other wifely occupations with unhealthy dispatch. She treats Jacinta as a daughter, not a daughter-in-law, ordering her boy to bed and Jacinta to pull up covers, pamper, stay close and treat him like a baby. It is Bárbara who distributes allowances, buys cufflinks, neckties, a stream of trifles, and who stocks up cigarettes for her boy, sniffing don Baldomero's cigars, laying away stacks of white shirts. Whiteness — clean, starched sheets and shirts — prompts in doña Bárbara a "real passion," suggesting her causal link to sterility. Infantile behavior shows how Juan himself usurps the place of Jacinta's unborn child. Fearing a competitor, he flatly tells Fortunata that he does not want his wife to bear a child. Moreno-Isla, deeply in love with Jacinta, takes the opposite view: to have a child with her would be the easiest thing in the world. It is not Jacinta who is the problem but her marriage: as Moreno says, to love a husband like Juan is like "feeding roses to a mule" — it goes against nature.

The usurpations extend to Jacinta herself. She becomes a stranger to her own perceptions, for social and familial conditioning have masked the emptiness and uselessness of her life. In her own thinking, she adheres to injurious self images — "such a shame that you can't *give* us something" is doña Bárbara's cruel intimation that sterility, like a bad business deal, is her fault. Even the process of thinking is carried out parsimoniously, as if coerced and contaminated by family notions of debit and credit. Lying awake, she takes thoughts out like coins to count them, testing to see if an idea is counterfeit. A young woman's mind imagined as a money box conveys perhaps the most damaging result of such an arranged marriage. Husband into child, mother into wife: identities and roles have merged into a kind of emotional incest, while the values assigned to its setting also change: an ample, comfortable house provides no room, no solace, no exit. The veneer of harmonious family relations peels away to show emptiness and sterility. These Jacinta must acknowledge as her own, clasping to her bosom the deficiencies of others, resolving stoically to bear them − her husband's disdain, the sorrow of childlessness. As pairs cross and triads overturn, Jacinta stands parallel, not opposed, to her fecund, martyred mother. She is also a *cordero* (a lamb) to the last, living out in reverse the lamb-like sacrificial labors of doña Isabel. Mothering has meant she will never be a mother.

In the Santa Cruz house, deprivation and abundance connect. Barbarita heaps up packages and narration keeps pace, adding "more and more details." Jacinta amasses emptiness as months and years pass. Barbarita presents a contented façade − her affability is constant, her figure untouched by time and her youth assured. Jacinta grows sadder, takes detours round an unfurnished nursery and sits sewing little shirts for Guillermina's orphanage. Barbarita's concerns stack the "upper story" of a divided page, as the narrator presents paragraphs chock-a-block with data that appear to assert her rule. By contrast, Jacinta's thoughts wind inwards and syntax vacillates, abounding with disclaimers, clauses, hesitations, ellipsis and questions, in order to *surround* the unspeakable matter of sterility. Barbarita, with her inherited, block-like ideas, believes in the perfect match of two paired marriages, while grieving Jacinta is gouged by the worm (*gusanillo*) of twin sorrows − her husband's separations and her childless state. All is disharmony despite asseverations of domestic tranquillity.

In Part 1, a small event, occurring outside the house on Pontejos Square, suggests how Jacinta's deprivation within abundance aligns her invisibly with Fortunata's world. One dark, rainy evening, she rushes home, flushed, angry, having been humiliated by her childless condition in her sister Candelaria's house. As she hurries past brightly illumined windows displaying the latest fashion, she turns towards Pontejos Square and hears a sound. She stops, listens: kittens cry, a desperate, high-pitched mewing that comes from a sewer (*absorbedero*), cries that transfix, penetrate, wound, evoking a maternal longing that cannot, ever, be assuaged. Deogracias, the janitor, squats and peers but nothing can be done. Rain comes down, the sewer glugs, spits filth, water gushes and the kittens drown. The little scene is symbolic of emotions suppressed, the murder of unwanted offspring, maternal ecstasy ("éxtasis de madre"), a thread snipped off ("prima de un violín"). God's countenance appears shaped as Thankless Stupidity (Deogracias), and there is a turbulence that stains, a craving coming from below, from sewers, from viscera ("desconsoladas entrañas"). Description picks out a "slit" ("hendidura") in "swollen" cement ("encintado"), and sketches the configuration of a nether world separated from the upper world, darkness from light and the sense of Dionysian chaos that rages beneath Apollonian order. Here, marked by the imagery of commonplace speech, is how Galdós's treatment of absorptive abundance − *absorbedero* − conveys mythic, unconscious material as part of the motif of sterility/fecundity. The symbolism condenses the motif as a *punto negro* in Jacinta. It is another one of her unspoken points of contact with Fortunata.

Jacinta's defective marriage, her childlessness and confinement within a family built upon inverted triads and usurped roles, provide the context for an extraordinary dream that occurs midway through Part 1. This dream, bound up with the question of sterility, crux of the relationship between Fortunata and Jacinta, does not, upon analysis, point to physical impairment, but rather shows a painfully repressed sexuality and how such unconscious feelings have been manipulated. It affirms in her what others, except Moreno, would deny: erotic energy. Flickering in her animated gestures and passion for Juan, that energy now surfaces in the dream.

The dream occurs while Jacinta, though unwilling to attend an opera, finds herself seated apart from Juan in the usual box, behind the bobbing heads of her younger sisters, advantageously displayed like goods at market. Coercion, subservience, theatrical appearances and separation from Juan, along with familiar components of setting and circumstance, combine to prompt a young wife's awareness that her husband's seat is empty, that he is absent, not there under the same roof to be close, to share. Here is an opera he acclaims, yet

it is contrary to her own taste. Like everything else in the
Santa Cruz household, Wagner, so in fashion, weighs upon
the uninstructed Jacinta who prefers, like Fortunata, light
Italian music, played by organ-grinders in the street.

Lonely and bored, Jacinta falls asleep and in her dream
the setting is ambivalent. She finds herself in a place that seems
like her house but is not really, for, as she unconsciously
senses, her house and marriage are not what they seem. The
walls, tapestried in flowered white satin, express that cluster
of cloth/money/sterility, so emblematic of don Baldomero's
early retirement, Juanito's parasitic idleness and Barbarita's
consumerism. The spongy, slippery white walls *surround*
Jacinta as she sits on a *pouff* lightly clad in a blue silk dressing
gown, reflecting chastity (the Virgin's robe) and sexuality
(Fortunata's gown of luscious blue velvet). A boy-child, naked
below the waist, climbs insistently up Jacinta's knees, his
flesh slipping on the watery silk, and repeatedly thrusts his
hand toward her breasts. At first she hesitates, as if constrained
by the unconscious awareness that she is, after all, in a public
place. Then the child, taking on a man's countenance, transfixes
her with a passionate stare and Jacinta melts, experiences
something akin to orgasm, expressed in Spanish as the sensation
of flesh throbbing inwardly, being torn away ("se le desgajaba
algo en sus entrañas"). Quickly, eagerly, she unbuttons her
gown, one, two, three, four buttons, five, a hundred, now
losing count as the cloth strains, "moans." She leans forward,
offering her breast, but the man-child freezes. His face and
lips have become white plaster, rasping, dusty, decayed.
Aghast, Jacinta draws back, awakens, looks up toward her
husband's seat ... but the fourth act is over, Juan is gone,
and she sees instead a strange, disconcerting picture that
completes the dream: Federico Ruiz, who had accompanied
Juan on his first trip to Paris, in ecstasy – eyes closed, lips
parted, as if to taste manna from heaven, a streaming liquid
likened to milk and honey, an image conveyed of a man-child
at breast (AG, 1974, 59). At that very moment, unbeknown
to Jacinta, Juan is with Fortunata and their dead child.

Dreams, the narrator says, are fictions that tell the truth.

Here is an ardent young woman who loves her husband. But with her he is a frozen man-child, calling for *teta* in rare moments of intimacy, otherwise indifferent as he seeks sex outside the house. His coldness to her is the stuff of gossip in all Madrid; even in Las Micaelas, Fortunata hears reports of his disdain. So within the silken confinements of the Santa Cruz house, Jacinta's sexual feelings have no place to go. Only a dream, experienced midway through an opera, tells the truth of her pain *and* the story of a dead child.

Triangular dialectics

A second, very different love triangle is established as Fortunata marries Maxi and renews her affair, developing the dialectic that will result in the reconciliation of the two women. As the title of Part 1 ("Juanito Santa Cruz") pivots on the title of Part 2 ("Maximiliano Rubín"), Galdós juxtaposes two lovers, two husbands: Juanito, high-born, handsome, a titled prince ("Delfín"), (but never a king) overshadowing the low-born Maxi, who makes his way into the world as a premature baby, possibly illegitimate. Orphaned and ugly, Maxi is presented as utterly "ordinary"; dubbed *Rubinius vulgaris* by his classmates, he is at the bottom of the pecking order and his minimal presence makes a joke of any reference to his Imperial namesake, Maximilian I.

As Part 2 begins, the narrator gives a few equivocal details about the Rubín family — their Jewish origins, Maxi's mother as a wanton woman, the dishonor of domestic violence and bankruptcy and the role of doña Lupe as surrogate mother. These facts will have a bearing on our understanding of Maxi's obsession with a woman's honor and of his madness. Historical antecedents, so prolixly asserted in Part 1, telescope to a single date as the narrator ticks off the fall of the throne (1868) and the failure of the family business. He also notes that creditors chop up bookshelves dating from the time of Velázquez, a small fact that hints at a subsequent change in the narrator's own painterly style: in describing Maxi, he will appear to have forsaken the balanced composition of a

Velázquez painting for the mannerist exaggerations of an El Greco.

Thus at the beginning of Part 2, everything appears to shrink as befits little Maxi and his origins among the petty bourgeoisie. At the same time, shrinkage, taken to extremes in the youngest Rubín son, becomes a metaphor for expansion, for exaggeration and the comically grotesque. A smashed-in nose, thinning hair, molars that amble about the mouth, pasty skin, pimpled cheeks, rickety knees, a torpid brain – misfortunes heap up in little Maxi. Abundance and deprivation connect, sketching a link with another character betrayed by fortune, Juan's childless wife Jacinta. Whereas the characterization of the Santa Cruz heir appeared to branch laterally through the great family tree, the characterization of Maxi evolves through more vertical oppositions – bodily ruin against imaginative richness, high hopes versus low aptitudes. Maxi, a blob-like "mollusk," re-imagines the world like a mystic. His manic thinking transports him to visionary realms where daydreams convey clues to a hidden fear of castration and impotence. As a teacher lectures on iodines in pharmacy class, Maxi envisages an empurpled soldier's sword, and the thought of doña Lupe buttoning his pants fills him with shame. Something unhinged agitates in such extremes, which point to the origins of madness in a complex of factors – the stain of maternal dishonor, his mother's death and her abandonment of him, leaving him an orphan, as well as his physical deformity. All told, however, something extraordinary starts developing as Maxi, struggling to gain a toehold in life, stumbles into manhood, snuffling vapors, suffering migraines. Then he meets Fortunata.

The encounter takes place in a casual way as a friend whispers the story of a young and reluctant prostitute in flight from misadventures in Paris, and arranges a visit. But one glance at Fortunata's face, illumined by a lamp, takes Maxi's breath away. From the start, dialectical terms characterize their relationship. She is a vision, not wholly of this world, while he is an insect, subhuman. She is a fallen woman, though pure in heart, whereas he is innocent, untried in love.

As the narrator passes these facts through the "inner doing" of their consciousness, what is ordinary becomes extraordinary; things, as if aroused, appear moved within themselves, taking on new life — a lamp flares up, Maxi's near-sighted gaze turns ecstatic and a prostitute takes flight as an "angelic" being. The scene, counterpart to the encounter on the stair, recalls El Greco as the narrator elongates proportions, stylizes the bird-egg motif and alters the image of the family tree, whose branching social connections have turned overnight into a fairy-tale image of a shining tree surging at the core of being. Deep in la Cava, Fortunata sucked a raw egg. In Part 2, up the social stair, the rawness of eggs is recalled in the bourgeois piggy bank that Maxi cracks open to assert his manhood. Silver spills upon the bed, gold coins glint like flecks of yolk, swimming amidst the whites: broken bits of red clay streak like blood. Maxi, reborn like Fortunata, becomes a man. He takes the money and sets up house with her.

They make an odd couple: she, strong, statuesque and of extraordinary beauty and he, a puny, misshapen man. Yet Maxi's love has transforming power, which is perceived as an indefinable aura about his face by a startled narrator. And Fortunata, at first diffident and skeptical, recognizes in her benefactor a profound decency. She wants to learn, to be respectable, and so tells her story of abuse and prostitution and of her enduring passion for Santa Cruz. Sincerity is her defining virtue. But as the new love triangle is shaped, positions start changing: Maxi, once a dreaming schoolboy, now acts as an attentive diagnostician. He insists on redeeming his beloved by controlling her destiny, standing tall *in loco parentis*. Fortunata, primitive in her ignorance, submits to his tutelage, laboring to read and write while instinctively acquiring the requisite social graces. Santa Cruz, however, remains the fixed angle, holding sway over her thoughts. While Fortunata rejoices at her new image in the mirror, Juan's presence persists in the reflection.

Galdós builds acute dialectical tensions into his new love triangle. As Fortunata and Maxi struggle to grow, we witness, in Gilman's words, the birth of consciousness in both antagonists.

The more adversarial the terms, the greater the potential for growth but the greater, too, the risk of madness as the mind vacillates between extremes. Over lunch, Fortunata's mind turns like a weathervane: it points south, toward images of domestic bliss and then turns north to face reality — Maxi's clotted eye, dribbling nose and asthmatic breathing as he spoons in stew. In between these is something new — preoccupation, effort, the rub of existence. Fortunata starts thinking and learns, for example, to distinguish gratitude from love, to perceive in the saintly Guillermina the brassy defiance of Mauricia *la Dura*, and to gain better access to language. By Part 4, she can best the joking Ballester at his own game, understand the irony of Nicolás Rubín's promotion and even outsmart doña Lupe, while as a fallen woman, always faced with Jacinta, she continually questions virtue, seeking to redefine who she, Fortunata, really is.

Maxi idolizes Fortunata. To gain her favors he reaches toward the sublime idea of redemption and, stretching too far, snaps. His impotence, her infidelity and the birth of the child send him into madness. At bottom Maxi is himself a child. He keeps suffering the primal shame of maternal dishonor and abuse whenever Fortunata rekindles his infantile craving for unconditional love, which she then betrays by her own unremitting passion for Santa Cruz. As a stunted being, the childlike Maxi manifests the feminine in his nature, whereas Mauricia *la Dura*, likened to Napoleon, flaunts masculine traits. Their dementia presses the narrator — a bourgeois *vulgaris* — to the limits of expression, so that he appears in his descriptions to keep placing these two terms of Galdós's theoretical equation at a further remove. This altered perspective is one reason for the narrator's cultivation of extremes that characterize Mauricia and Maxi, their relationship to Fortunata and their madness. For in relation to these extremes the characterization of Fortunata moves to the center of the equation, and what is most natural about her hovers at the "perfect point of balance" between objective and subjective modes. In this way naturalness, associated with balance, acquires the attributes of what is most real, hence of most value, and Fortunata comes to embody the stated aim of Galdós's art.

Imagined loves

Narrator and Barbarita

In Part 1 the narrator shows a keen eye for women, especially Barbarita. At the age of fifteen she is a darling, her trim figure firmly rounded, her pretty face blossoming, ready for love. The sketch carries the freshness of an eye-witness account, although his personal, social acquaintance will date expressly from 1870, when Barbarita is a respectable matron of fifty-two. In that moment the voltage goes up: Barbarita, strolling on don Baldomero's arm, incites an erotically charged description that likens her to a ripe plum, swollen and sticky, with sugary juices oozing from splits in the skin. As this narrator states, confesses and exclaims his desire, the tripled denotation of the verb *decir* shifts mood from indicative to subjunctive. His eyes caress her figure, slender even without a corset; his mind imagines a romantic idyll; pauses – *puntos* – mark that breath taken when he and Juanito stand astonished as Fortunata steps toward the stair. In this way, the meeting between the narrator and Barbarita represents another encounter that alludes to "birth" as we glimpse two emerging new selves: Barbarita's sexual persona, repressed as controlling energy beneath a respectable exterior, and the narrator's donjuanesque disposition, not unlike that of Juanito Santa Cruz.

Slowly the narrator develops. The perception of Barbarita's tyranny within the household, the venal corruptions of shopping and her indulgence of Juan's caprices incline our sympathies to Jacinta. Barbarita becomes the formidable matron *doña* Bárbara. the narration acquires a satiric edge as scenes are staged: doña Bárbara appears in the doorway to announce the menu for lunch in administrative jargon. In the scene, the manservant Blas tucks up a little tray, sets out fat, succulent birds for Juan's sickbed, while in the text diminutives like

Juanito, niño, alternating with *doña,* appear to reiterate the rocking of a cradle that nurtures the oral greediness of a grown son, now swathed in bedclothes. As Juan relishes the trussed-up birds, we recognize the child who caught birds in a net with Estupiñá grown into the man who refused Fortunata's raw egg, asked for the teat and appeared in Jacinta's dream.

By Part 4 doña Bárbara ceases to appear as a ruling presence except when the child is born, and the narrator obliquely associates her with Aurora. Small facts link the families of Aurora and the entrepreneurial señora de Santa Cruz, marking their concern with appearances. Both women prefer distinctly white fabrics – starched shirts and tablecloths for Bárbara, bridal outfits and baby layettes in Aurora's boutique. Each is an astute shopper and manager. Bárbara, recognizing talent in Aurora, steps across the street every day to watch her work, delighted with her style – says Guillermina, even as Aurora takes up with Juan. Barbarita, a ripe, juicy plum not unlike a fruit cocktail ("compota"), is analogous to Aurora, coarsely good-looking ("guapota"), whose favorite dessert is a dish of stewed plums ("compota"). Each has sticky fingers, each steals, each betrays her own sex in order to retain ascendancy over don Juan, the *punto negro* of persisting love triangles.

Juan and Aurora

Aurora's liaison with Juanito is crucial to the plot. In Part 2, she appears indirectly, framed in a photograph of the Samaniego sisters, their arms enlaced. This initial glimpse picks out the motifs of enlacement and framing that will surround Aurora's every gesture as in Part 4 she steps from photograph to parlor, arm enlaced around Fortunata, her supposed friend. Aurora cleverly frames their conversations, setting the scene, taking possession of Fortunata's secrets, stealing her lover and inventing the love story of Jacinta and Moreno that allegedly cuckolds Santa Cruz.

Aurora's own "enlacements" – her position in the boutique, owed to family connections, and her liaison with Juan – make up the story Maxi uses as a weapon in his attempt to "assassinate" the faithless Fortunata. Fortunata, in turn, lacerates Aurora's face on the floor of Madrid's most fashionable foreign shop. Now the notion of frames and enlacements at which Aurora is so adept appear in an ironic light, as her treachery brings about her own dishonor and a final embrace between Fortunata and Jacinta. As if to anticipate this irony, the narrator, in a casual figure of speech that alludes to frames ("Aquí cuadra decir"), frames *her*, taking care to set up Aurora as a foil to Fortunata. For in contrast to Fortunata's strong, shapely figure, Aurora is anemic, spongy, not fit or firm. The rolled flesh of her upper arms squeezes the seam of her sleeves, denoting passion pressed to the petty edges of mercantile ambition. Her bursting, bulky bosom, short neck, arranged hairdo and strictly aligned skirt (no patterns or variegated colors) suggest mulish origins, the sense of harnesses pulled hard. Aurora, like Barbarita, specializes in *calzas*, arms entwining, hands touching, fingers sticking as she offers Fortunata candied yolks, not a raw egg, all the while conversing, corrupting, configuring a new, treacherous love triangle between Jacinta, Moreno-Isla and Juan.

In demeanor and deportment, adapted to the French manner, Aurora represents the "dawn" of opportunity for working women. In contrast to stallkeepers, seamstresses, cooks, maids and the factory girls whom Jacinta sees in Barcelona, Aurora has independent means. Her dressed-up style of streetwalking is decent, respectable. Widowed with no children, bilingual and skilled in dress design, management and sales, she appears liberated from patriarchal traditions of female domestic and familial duty. But with Aurora, in work as in friendship, things are not what they seem. She owes employment to a former lover, Moreno-Isla, and to her cousin Pepe Samaniego, married to Jacinta's sister. Family relations — that reliable Madrid grapevine — are what count. At home, while not constrained by a Catholic upbringing, Aurora at the age of thirty must still defer to doña Casta, escaping to the balcony for conversation, lying to protect her liaison with Santa Cruz. Seduced by rich, frivolous don Juans, first Moreno (who entered her house as His Holy Majesty), then Juanito (who stepped, heaven-sent, into Jacinta's parlor), Aurora remains a kept woman, perpetuating traditional roles and abuses.

Moreno-Isla, Jacinta and Fortunata

Aurora's seducer, don Manuel Moreno-Isla, is an expatriate, an island ("isla") to himself, although as a banker of wealth and prominence he often appears as one of the many guests in the Santa Cruz house. By Part 4, Aurora's vengeful whispers have linked Jacinta to Moreno, whose passion for Santa Cruz's wife stands in analogy to Fortunata's for Juan. These new pairs and triangles place Fortunata and Jacinta within a moral perspective that reconciles them, dignifying their desire for a child. That child, first conceived as Fortunata's "madcap idea" ("pícara idea") and brought to term, so to speak, by Jacinta's "whirlwind of thoughts" ("ciclón de pensamientos"), belongs also to Moreno. In Part 3 a simple structural device, which Galdós learned from Cervantes, appears to "hatch" that child in Moreno's house: the title "La idea ... la pícara idea" opens a chapter that depicts a love scene not where Fortunata lives or having anything to do with her but in Moreno's house, where he encounters Jacinta. We hear a rustle of skirts, the sound of kisses and see a small, winged, "angelic hand," plump as a dove, alight upon Moreno's shoulder as he sits enthralled, all thought transfixed by the dove-like Jacinta. Fortunata is faraway, alien to the scene, yet her "idea" of parenthood circles, as it were, above the heads of Moreno and Jacinta, and later reappears among those "dove-ideas" that flock to Moreno's mind as he thinks of Jacinta just before he dies.

In Part 4 the second chapter, titled "Insomnia," develops this story of Moreno's obsessive love and his unspoken kinship to Fortunata. An interior monologue, displaying a remarkably modern stream-of-consciousness, unravels the thoughts that culminate in those "dove ideas" that bring on successive waves of blood, confirming *succession* in the precise moment of death. The manner of his death presages hers, and it is no coincidence that he owns the building in la Cava where she dies as she contemplates her infant son. A similar stylistic shaping, conveyed by shifts in narrative focus, further discloses the temperamental affinity between these two characters, who at first appear so at odds and who come from opposite ends of the social spectrum. Yet as each presses to the limits of feeling, Galdós dignifies their story by controlling distance – slowing the pace, letting them speak for themselves and executing a final shift in narrative focus, which at the end pans out almost cinematographically to give an objective glimpse of their faces, his blood-stained, hers ivory-white, with two or three flies on her brow. Each dies in a gush of blood, refusing to moderate their passion, and the prescriptions of modern medicine (Moreno-Rubio) and mentors (Feijoo) are as nothing before the wave. Each is an orphan, each imagines a child and each gives birth: Fortunata conceives a dove-child and Moreno, thinking of Jacinta, retrieves in himself a lost child, imagines "dove-ideas" and persists in his passion, which he prizes more than the middle-class notion of virtue. Society has no use for Fortunata, but neither will it tolerate tumultuous feeling in one of its most refined products, a banker who protests against the founding, matriarchal Trujillo "bar of steel."

Feijoo and Fortunata

In Part 3, Evaristo González Feijoo, an acquaintance of Moreno-Isla, meets Fortunata as she lays siege to the house on Pontejos Square and watches Bárbara and Jacinta step to a carriage in a blur of silks, furs and jewels. Feijoo also calls a carriage, and thus begins what will be the warmest relationship between the sexes in the novel. As lover and mentor of Fortunata, Feijoo follows Maxi, Nicolás and doña Lupe in his attempt to reform her. He acts as Pygmalion to his Galatea, eager to cut facets and polish that "diamond in the rough." Feijoo is also the apologist for Fortunata – the benevolent, educated man who formulates a rational justification for free love and for Fortunata's conviction that love rights every wrong. As self-appointed creator, Feijoo replicates authorial functions to some degree. He recasts his artistic enterprise into a specifically literary context, "reading" Fortunata's thoughts and writing the script for her eventual reconciliation with Maxi.

The seasoned Feijoo appears as an authorial, and in part, autobiographical projection, speaking for Galdós on politics, charity and the relationship of the sexes. He also insists on an ethic of conciliation and compromise, and on the "realism" of things brought into balance. He tries to develop in Fortunata a sense of compromise between things as they are and what she desires, compromise being his bourgeois equivalent of Galdós's theoretical equation. But Feijoo strays too close to the pretensions of a don Juan and, like his adversary Santa Cruz, receives a kind of retributive justice particular to his gift for reasoning and for arranging other people's lives. It is as if Galdós recognized an alter ego in Feijoo and acknowledged a wrong done in the depiction of Feijoo's senility − as the episode concludes he is a deaf old don Juan who plays with kittens. At the beginning Feijoo encounters Juanito at Fortunata's house − at the end, as if to recall Santa Cruz's own preference for preening, cat-like prostitutes, felines usurp Fortunata's place at Feijoo's bedside.

Feijoo occupies a pivotal position in the novel. Certain details in café scenes hint at his acquaintance with Maxi's wife and lay the groundwork for his role in the fourth chapter of Part 3. The chapter, titled "A Lesson in Practical Philosophy," occurs near the center of the novel, between the end of Fortunata's second liaison and her reconciliation with Maxi. The branching tables recall the family tree, and the café, all smoke and mirrors, cooks up stories. Among them is Fortunata's liaison with Feijoo, the only character connected to all three social spheres who possesses the authority needed to create another dimension in her, to restore her marriage and to insure her financial independence. As a retired military officer he moves outside Madrid's mercantile districts, and, though not subject to buying and selling, he is close to the Santa Cruz circle. Feijoo's entrée with the petty bourgeosie is assured through his service in the same regiment as Jáuregui, doña Lupe's late husband; she imagines her widowhood consoled by his amorous advances. Feijoo becomes acquainted with Fortunata and other women of *pueblo* origin through his conversation partner in cafés, Maxi's brother Juan Pablo Rubín.

The narrator concentrates on Feijoo's benevolence and charm, his physical cleanliness and enlightenment in order to emphasize decency and respectability. He wishes to stress the idea that as a wealthy, aristocratic bachelor, Feijoo at sixty-nine is no opportunistic old man with dirty ideas (*viejo verde*), despite his affairs, his unconventional views of love and marriage and his unseemly, adulterous May–December liaison with Fortunata, forty-five years his junior. She experiences no genuine passion for her partner and at first submits unwillingly to the arrangement. From the start, as Feijoo declares, sexuality is a factor in their relations and a prime reason, we suspect, for his abrupt physical decline. But the narrator glosses over the physical aspect of their relations, emphasizing instead a paternal affection that Feijoo himself sees as appropriate to a father–daughter relationship.

Feijoo proceeds with tact and discretion. He rents rooms in an outlying neighborhood, procures a respectable maid, keeps Fortunata dressed modestly and encourages her self-respect. His plan is to restore honor and social decency through appearances, minimizing her status as a fallen woman. He wants to let her breathe and to return to her natural ways. While he proposes to treat her stubbornness, breaking in that "mule," his artistic vision of Fortunata is neither new nor "fictional." Rather it respects what is – and always was – her real animal nature ("res"), her primitive ways. What Feijoo does is to shape Fortunata's native rawness, which for him is a thing of beauty although rawness, like oozing egg whites, had proved repulsive to Juanito. Guided by Feijoo, Fortunata's beauty, born (*nata*) of chance (*fortuna*), returns to its original state with arms akimbo, *pueblo* speech alive on the tongue, flesh firm and rounded, body exuding strength and health. Sincerity is the only house rule. Feijoo shows Fortunata how to fit passion to social norms, manage money and live reconciled to an unloved husband. He teaches her, in sum, to survive a drab and dispiriting household routine, while always maintaining composure.

The aim of Feijoo's course in practical ethics is Fortunata's independence, which he attempts to effect, quite ironically, by controlling her behavior, by doing her thinking, by making decisions as to where they live, what she does, what she wears, whom she meets. Only in cooking is she allowed to choose. Fortunata sees herself as a working-class girl, eager to pack a lunch, raise children, sew, scrub, polish, be *pueblo*. But according to Feijoo's plan, work is not an option because her predicament as a fallen woman, obligated to accept a man's protection, is presented as unalterable fact, *la realidad*. But is it? Everywhere women work – as maids, seamstresses, stallsellers – hard work, but respectable work, and work which Fortunata knows how to do. *La realidad* results not because it *has* to happen but because it *ought* to happen, in line with Feijoo's desires, and the narrator, ever alert to a beautiful woman, concurs as he bows to the inevitable – no joking with *la realidad*, he says, edging closer to breathe Feijoo's cologne and delight in Fortunata's star-dusted lashes. Why does Feijoo propose the plan? Astonished (like Santa Cruz) by the raw energy of her beauty, Feijoo, who is retired from the military with nothing to do but gab in cafés, finds the project of cultivating Fortunata irresistible. So he buys her a Singer sewing machine – *not* for work but entertainment – and organizes her life, thus maintaining her as a kept woman. In contrast to Moreno-Isla, who after trifling with Aurora nonetheless insists that she be employed as floor manager of Samaniego's boutique, Feijoo does not marshal his considerable resources to establish Fortunata in some form of paid work.

Feijoo's lessons in bourgeois practicality ultimately fail, and the narrator uses a bourgeois discourse to mark the irony of the failure – Feijoo is a "creditor" of Fortunata's affection, and the restoration of the marriage moves with the precision of a timepiece as members of the Rubín family turn into his puppets. In the end, for all his reasoning, Feijoo appears to be more in love with his idea than with practical results, so that his seeming reasonableness produces only pandemonium. Thus a burdened Fortunata must take responsibility for the chaos in her marriage brought about by her renewed affair, although the restoration of the marriage, Feijoo's handiwork, is actually what causes Maxi's "fermented" jealousy and psychotic break with reality. While Feijoo undoubtedly is the best of Fortunata's reformers, benevolent reason alone cannot solve the difficulties of life, and, as if in retribution, Galdós (not the narrator) metes out that exquisite punishment of senility: Feijoo becomes as a child, drooling, napping, while Fortunata at his bedside holds the spoon; her maternal solicitude makes the medicine go down.

In this way Galdós shrinks Feijoo's authority to something life-size, something even smaller than life – remembered bits and pieces that Fortunata can take in and use in her own way, accomplishing what Ballester calls the "digestive work of the spirit." And she does this to perfection in the closing scene of Part 3, once again in a carriage and solicited by don Juan. Pressed to renew the affair with Santa Cruz, she recalls Feijoo's counsel, now countering Juan as an equal. Each advocates caution and each recites lines from a popular play, he caressing her thigh, she digging her nails into his flesh, now motivated less by passion than by her own "madcap idea" – a "pícara idea" that becomes a kind of "planned parenthood," resulting in the birth of the child. The child is named in part for Feijoo, and death itself harbors another connecting sign: as Ballester and Ponce leave Fortunata's burial, Feijoo's funeral procession enters the cemetery.

Segismundo Ballester

Part 4 opens with Segismundo Ballester, pharmacist in doña Casta's establishment on Ave María Street, where Fortunata's story returns to the more mixed circumstances of daily life. The notion of mixtures, in art as well as life, appears to hold sway as Ballester makes up pharmaceutical compounds, combines music and medicine and convenes a literary circle where friends discuss the aesthetics of realism. The association of such theoretical debates about "mixed styles" with the mixed traits of Ballester's personality and profession suggest how this character, in contrast to Feijoo, approximates the author's narrative persona. His name combines the heroic (Segismundo) with the plainer notion of a sharpshooter (Ballester), and his character and social class present a mix of qualities. Although Ballester has a university education and knows (like Galdós) the music of Rossini and Beethoven, he keeps close to his working-class origins. He dresses up for his sister's wedding to a member of the Santa Cruz circle, dresses down for work, wearing scuffed-up slippers. Blunted features, a spreading figure and spiky hair denote looseness, a disposition hospitable to growth: Ballester can stretch, take in, embrace, comfort, talk sense. He shows no hard edges, like Guillermina, no dandified elegance like Santa Cruz and Moreno and no compact correctness, like the clean-shaven Feijoo, although as this elderly gentleman changes from lover to father he becomes more unkempt in appearance, more authentic ... more like Ballester.

If the characterization of Feijoo (and Santa Cruz) approaches the narrator's own disposition, Ballester, a slovenly lover, stands closest to that rumpled man in Sorolla's portrait of Galdós. Something of the spoiled child persists in Feijoo, whereas Ballester's occasional extravagance and silliness become the mark of a mature man, steady in work, loyal in friendship, discreet and magnanimous in his love for Fortunata. He takes risks, putting his livelihood on the line as he attends her pregnancy, only to lose his job at the pharmacy. Feijoo dictates advice as if he were already in possession of the "truth," whereas Ballester does what he terms "the digestive work of the spirit." He respects the elements that make up compounds – not for him a quick fix like those *panaceas* urged by doña Lupe or the abstractions that obsess Maxi. To mark these virtues Galdós associates Balleter with the great master Cervantes by alluding to episodes from the *Quijote* – like the priest and the barber, this good man snatches noxious books from Maxi, promising him fertile isles in reward for good behavior.

Santa Cruz stays under wraps; Feijoo, snug in his niche, sits in cafés and plays cards with Fortunata. Ballester stands tip-toe at the door, moves from front to back, mixes a mustard plaster, sniffs a greasy jar, all the while advising, comforting and quieting panic in the household. Among the male characters, Ballester shows an unusual range of emotional responses as he worries and weeps; for him, sentience is paramount. Pharmaceutical art, he says, must "wound" the sensitive side of humanness. In descriptions of Ballester gerunds predominate, expressing the animation of his whole person. Everything *passes through* Ballester, whereas Santa Cruz, Moreno and Feijoo ride horses, rent carriages, take strolls and *pass by*. Santa Cruz falls from a horse, Moreno falls from a burro, Feijoo falls into senility, but the generous Ballester only falls from favor as he assists Fortunata. Santa Cruz buys silks and satins, Feijoo sends roses and Moreno lets a narcissus fall from his glove, but Ballester brings medicines, arranges Quevedo's midwifery, sits in vigil, rejoices in birth, acts as buffer, converses, jokes, encourages and protects.

Unlike Santa Cruz, who toys cruelly with Fortunata, or Maxi, who dreams of her as an ideal, and unlike Feijoo, who cuts and polishes, Ballester respects Fortunata as she is. He accepts her mulish behavior and eschews the harness. He loves precisely her mix of qualities and attributes, understands how these evolve and sees her always ascending. She is angelic in her own way, an angel who keeps misfiring ("un ángel que hacía disparates"), not perfect and even dangerous, but ever sublime; a Biblical goddess, virginal, chaste – *la casta Susana*. Through the characterization of Ballester Galdós suggests what might have been – a modest pharmacist as husband to Fortunata. He imagines them as a new pair joined to another pair, Jacinta and Moreno. Now the couples become a subversive set of two-by-fours that help build the reconciling embrace between the two women.

In Part 1, family ties expand and Juanito's *novela* contracts – Fortunata was, he says, a "parenthesis", a trifling page. In Parts 2 and 3 family history contracts whereas the "parenthesis" cracks open and "eggs" hatch as Maxi breaks his piggy bank,

Feijoo feathers a love nest and Fortunata pursues her dove-idea. Now in Part 4, the process telescopes as family history – Ballester's biography – stands summed up *in* a parenthesis, while *on* Ave María Street and *in* la Cava, conception, annunciation and birth bring the dove-child, ending Fortunata's life to conceive it anew in literary form. If a petty, degraded don Juan started his *novela* on the great stone stair, if Feijoo added a chapter on free love, Ballester *regente*, holds sway over a developing, quijotesque life-story that he, as author and literary critic, reinvents as a "play or a novel" toward the end.

Rebels and reformers

With the decline of don Juans, female energies rise in Old Madrid. Revolution and rising expectations pass through the three social classes to characterize three particularly strong, masterful women – Guillermina Pacheco, *la santa*, Doña Lupe, *la ministra* and Mauricia *la Dura*. All share certain masculine traits. Guillermina's speech is direct, inflexible, commanding. She represents the Church Militant and strides as a soldier in Christ. Doña Lupe is also something of a campaigner in the field, marshaling, contesting and inspecting her regimented household. The narrator mentions her "mocedad" – a "boyish" youth that recalls ballads about the Cid (*Las mocedades de Rodrigo*) – and we sense how an epic grandeur, cut to the cloth of the petty bourgeoisie, resonates in doña Lupe's excesses, even in her upper lip that prickles with an adolescent moustache. Her temper is volcanic and she possesses a novelist's gift of gab. We see her combining gossip with accounting, sorting numbers and sorting out stories. Mauricia *la Dura* is the spitting image of Napoleon – bobbed hair, high cheekbones, blazing eyes, aquiline nose, arms akimbo, stepped-up boots, freebooting arrogance. Her gutter speech employs the coarsest invectives.

Introduced midway through Part 2, Mauricia occupies the center of the novel. The episode of her illness and death brings together Fortunata and Jacinta, doña Lupe and Guillermina, and the scenes highlight the divisiveness that occurs within and among women who must live constrained in a society that prohibits their full use of heart, body and brain. In Old Madrid no precedents exist for a lay saint like Guillermina or a female minister of finance like doña Lupe or a street-smart, sexually liberated female philosopher like Mauricia, and, as these women struggle to express thought and feeling, they often seem eccentric or violent. Guillermina rejects convent life for the street and on occasion appears as a witch. Doña lupe knows she will explode if unable to vent her urge to manage. Mauricia sits on a garbage heap headed for the gutter, while childlessness ages Jacinta and Fortunata avenges wrongs by becoming as "bad" as she can. In depicting the four women Galdós delineates the conflictive psychology particular to their sex and to children, with whom women are often equated and to whom powerful men like Santa Cruz assign an inferior moral code.

Guillermina, of Trujillo origin and Moreno money, is a religious social reformer who moves from Barbarita's parlor on Pontejos Square to the slums of Mira el Río, where she attends the moribund Mauricia *la Dura* and ultimately confronts Fortunata. Mauricia's mother had done the ironing for the Pacheco household, which provides a childhood connection between Mauricia — alcoholic, prostitute, satanic rebel — and the saintly, aristocratic Guillermina. Between these social extremes we find doña Lupe, who sits at her window, watches Guillermina pass by and senses a kinship in their ability to found, build, manage, make money, make policy and push people around. *La santa* is *la ministra*'s alter ego. Each practices disguise, the one falsifying origins in her humble dress, the other falsifying a breast — doña Lupe possesses only one breast as a result of a mastectomy, and the cotton substitute, as unfeeling as her ruthless interest in money, is not unlike the insolence Guillermina displays when soliciting funds from rich and poor alike. Each is bound by family ties, each reveres social decorum and each attempts to reform Fortunata. Both are friends of Mauricia, who lived in Guillermina's house and who now sells the shawls, jewels and silver-plate that doña Lupe has acquired in her partnership with the usurer Torquemada. Presiding from a chair crowned with hand-crocheted anti-macassars, doña Lupe aspires to social prominence. She would give her right arm (right breast) to wave a muff among furs at *la santa*'s charity benefits.

The theme of charity mediates between the three women. As noted by Braun and Ortiz Armengol, Guillermina is modeled on the exemplary figure of doña Ernestina Manuel de Villena, who founded an orphanage in 1880. King Alfonso XII himself laid the cornerstone, and the orphanage remained standing in Madrid (Claudio Coello, 100) until December 1973. Doña Ernestina, much admired by Galdós, died in 1885 as *Fortunata and Jacinta* was being written, and in his "Memorias" (1916) Galdós declared she deserved sainthood ("merece a todas luces la canonización," 1663). The characterization of Guillermina also draws on mysticism and the founding enterprises of Santa Teresa and other great abbesses of the Renaissance. She combines traditions of chastity and social reform with contemporary middle-class values: a quasi-wifely insistence on family life with a regard for law, order and patriarchal rule. Guillermina also has a keen eye for a bargain and the cleverness of a rogue as she pick-pockets wallets among male guests, exacts a profit from Izquierdo over the sale of *el Pituso* and marches up to King Amadeo to wrest *reales* for her orphanage.

At first this mixture of traits and behaviors characterizes Guillermina in a balanced, positive way. At dinner she refuses fancy food but rejects convent life – she will tolerate no submission to superiors. She rebels against insipid social circles, frightening the ladies, yet adheres to traditional family mores. Always a dreamer, she keeps a practical eye on business; hers is a strict, even fanatical faith, yet full of liveliness and genuine spirituality. Toward the end, however, the balance breaks down. When petitioning funds, kings and paupers may be equal in Guillermina's eyes, but, as she admonishes Fortunata, the skirts of this fallen woman dare not *touch* the silks and satins of a lady like Jacinta. On occasion, more tumultuous feelings break through, and we note a startling symmetry between the virginal Guillermina *la santa* and the prostitute Mauricia *la Dura*. Fortunata perceives this similarity, confusing them in her mind as Guillermina *la Dura* and *doña* Mauricia.

As an untamed erotic force Mauricia *la Dura* brings into focus those subliminal feminine drives that exist in conflict with a patriarchal society. These drives surface in the entrepreneurial resolve of Jacinta's mother, Isabel Cordero, who ran a business and managed a huge household, and yet who remained subservient to her husband, even though all he ever did was fold the great Manila shawl. The conflict appears in doña Lupe's ambitions, mocked by the narrator, and in Guillermina's religious social work, which most men consider an unseemly annoyance. Both women find an echo in Mauricia, a storm-center of opposing forces, for whom *la santa* and *la ministra* are stable points of origin and social interaction. As Mauricia holds the convent at bay with a barrage of stones, her bared breast incites feelings that flicker in the eccentricities of the nuns, strike in Guillermina's flinty tongue, burst as a "bomb" in doña Lupe, burn as a tiger's eye in Fortunata and smolder viscerally in Jacinta, who takes Mauricia's daughter as her protegée. Electricity, thunderclaps and surging water appear associated with *la Dura*, whose name denotes the harsh, brassy behavior of one who voices the collective feminine unconscious, marked symbolically by the image of watery exchanges in her dialogues with Fortunata as each recalls "impure" thoughts about the past.

In effect, friendship with Mauricia becomes an important factor in the development of Fortunata's consciousness. Before their encounter in Las Micaelas, Fortunata's mind turned as a weathervane. Once she takes in Mauricia's gutter speech, sexuality and rage, that weathervane goes to work, as the disk outside the convent, turning in the wind, starts pumping water from the well. Now her mind labors like a swarm of worker ants, the image denoting how she retrieves, stores and transforms impressions into ideas, and both *la Dura* and *la santa* surge in her spirit like alternating currents of energy. Mauricia speaks for love, for stormy feelings that streak like "glacial lightning" in Fortunata's soul, and after she dies Fortunata

reimagines her as Guillermina. The duality of *la Dura* and
la santa, passing through her mind, appears to link her basic,
passionate nature with a newly forming, more idealized self.

The challenge Mauricia presents to Madrid's patriarchy is
symbolically shown in the chapel dream that occurs midway
through Part 2. In that dream Mauricia, in an alcoholic haze,
commits the blasphemy of robbing the chalice and eating the
Host – an imagined act of rebellion that nonetheless, as the
narrator says, becomes real through the immensity of the
will. The motif of maternal yearning recalls Jacinta's dream,
as Mauricia, deprived of her own child, identifies with the
Virgin as *Mater Dolorosa*. But whereas the dreaming Jacinta
sat primly at the opera and tried to unbutton her dress, *la
Dura*'s dream is more like an earthquake, shaking foundations,
opening doors. She grasps the chalice and holds it triumphant,
empowered by the golden spikes that encircle a virile godhead.
Placing the Host on her tongue, she swallows and silences
the voice that – like a woman's – cajoles and cries in protest.
Momentarily surfeited with supreme male power, she goes
on a rampage, hurling stones and spitting lewd cat-calls about
nuns who toss their sheets with lascivious French priests,
making do in their depravity with home-grown products like
don León Pintado. God himself is cuckolded. And just before
Mauricia dies, her rantings coarsen with remembrances of the
erotic content of this dream. Doña Lupe, recounting particulars,
registers something of that erotic feeling in Mauricia, who
craves the chalice as a sexual partner, caressing the "handsome"
Host with her eyes, snatching the chalice from the altar and
plunging it into her "trunk."

The chapel dream has metonymic force. As Braun notes, its
components reiterate the plot: a noble mother (the Virgin)
deprived of her child. An unknown woman (Mauricia), of low
birth and status, recovers and returns that child. Jacinta, in
the Virgin's blue robe, dreams of a lost child. Fortunata,
surging from below, bequeaths that child to her. The chapel
dream also bears the mark of Galdós's own liberal protest.
In a society kept closed by a powerful Church, blasphemy
pushes open the shutters and calls for the birth of human

rights. Mauricia's assault suggests this idea and takes it to
a lunatic edge as she opens the door of the sanctuary and tries
to return the Child, which prefigures the birth of Fortunata's
child and its "return" to Jacinta.

Lastly, Mauricia's chapel dream conveys the idea that what
is taboo − crazy thoughts, female sexuality − has a place
at the very center of things, and that this craziness and female
eroticism are part of the human condition. While Galdós,
noted for reticence, gives us little sexual detail − Ballester
is the only man shown to kiss Fortunata, and this effusive
act occurs only at her death − a full range of human sexuality
is nevertheless suggested. In Mauricia's rantings we see how
a huge, limitless, incredible absurdity nonetheless finds a
home within the "immeasurable mold of the human mind."
Though unlettered and snarling in speech, Mauricia draws
forth the narrator's most considered reflections about what
is real in the world of the realist novel.

Thus the narrator registers how something new and disconcerting happens when the aristocratic *Miss* Guillermina
comes in contact with *pueblo* female sexuality. As a young
woman, reacting in grief to the death of her mother, Guillermina
had dedicated herself to God. Now, as Mauricia lies dying, she
embraces, kisses and craves the God that Father Nones brings
in a snow-white wafer. Mauricia lies as in a trance. Guillermina
presses close, cheek against cheek, lips to lips, kissing, crying,
at the moment that Father Nones places the white wafer on
the dying woman's tongue. The scene, for a split second,
becomes almost erotically charged as Guillermina exhorts
Mauricia to confess and spit out sins. When *la Dura* resists,
disoriented, Guillermina grabs a bottle, presses liquor between
Mauricia's parted lips and awaits the confession of faith as
if to appropriate that faith for herself. We recall how in Las
Micaelas the little hunchback nun, Sor Marcela meted out
brandy, only a thimbleful, only enough to comfort and restore
balance. But Guillermina, craving God, fills Mauricia's glass
to the brim.

In the convent a rebellious Mauricia stones *la santa*, as if
the religious reformer were an adulterous woman. After

Mauricia's death Guillermina heaps on Fortunata's head a shower of cruel taunts and accusations, stunning the girl "as if a basket of stones were emptied over her skull." By contrast Sor Marcela, humping along on a wooden leg, exacts discipline with love. There is something rageful, even erotic, agitating in the spirit of this Christian soldier − *la capitana generala* − who exalts abjection, craves sacrifice and dictates cleanliness as she wades in excremental filth, preparing Mauricia's body, and as she exacts of Fortunata a sacrifice of a magnitude she herself desires. Sor Marcela's compassion comes from experience − the little nun takes a puff on Mauricia's cigarette and comforts a soul, whereas Guillermina, clasping the cross to her breast as Mauricia had clasped the chalice, wants to taste with her own lips the life spark of a rebel who once dreamed of eating her God.

We now suspect crookedness in the straightforward Guillermina. Yes, she knits little sweaters in Barbarita's parlor, but she never mingles with children, comforts them or enjoys their company, and affectionate, filial terms ("hijo") are scantily dispensed, not to children, but, more patronizingly, to childlike adults, like the brutish Izquierdo. Anxious to buy *el Pituso* for Jacinta, *la santa* plays the role of broker − the 4000 reales, saved by bargaining, making up her "commission." She accedes to staging an interview with Fortunata, hiding Jacinta, and thus *acts* as a confessor. When the real *Pituso* is born Guillermina invades the bedroom, articulating the half-recognized wish that Fortunata should die, while telling Jacinta that both women should proceed circumspectly, lest they look like intriguers from Ido's novel. In her altercations with the rebellious spirit of a dying Fortunata, now viewed as *la diabla*, Guillermina *la santa* does become an intriguer, living out the script of Ido's novel as she attempts to return the child to its "rightful" mother.

By now epithets like *diabla* and *santa* have become ironic misnomers as Guillermina insists on ritual purification, while Fortunata knows that her shining idea suffices. *La santa* dismisses the gift of the child as a *rasgo* − merely an impulsive act − whereas *la diabla* knows her generous gift redeems both herself and her rival. Redemption lies beyond the narrower religious faith of Guillermina, who fails to perceive that *la diabla* is, as she claims, angelic. Unable to apprehend the spirituality of Fortunata's last act, *la santa* herself remains earthbound. Thus, in the end, it is Fortunata *la diabla* who manifests the mystery, the limitlessness, of reality in Galdós's greatest novel.

Chapter 3

Metaphors of mind

The analogical matrix

When describing realism in the novel Galdós stresses neither fact nor fiction but likeness/comparison. His avowed aim was not to depict an object but to *surround* it, so to speak, by establishing dialectical patterns that build a sense of character, sketch in dot-images or formulate imagistic progressions. As the characters experience events, sometimes glossing their own story, their thoughts and words appear against a background of voices that resonate within a nexus of relations. The narrator develops these relations by passing known facts through told stories, imparting a visual and auditory sense of Galdós's equation, of things tacitly compared and maintained in balance.

This nimble touch likens the narrator at times to Juanito Santa Cruz, also adept at analogies in story-telling. What Hafter calls a kind of ironic reprise fades in and out among narrative styles, in this case exposing Juanito, the very man the narrator intends to punish. As Hafter says, internal repetitions, a variety of verbal echoes and the mirroring of one character in another reveal, "in varied pairings the novelist's irony has fashioned, more about themselves and about the surrounding reality than they themselves understand" (MH, 233). In *Fortunata and Jacinta*, then, as Rodgers has observed of *Miau*, irony and analogy become the two prongs of an instrument that catches hold of an object and renders it real in terms of the novel. Whereas the two stories of married women evolve within what is common, ordinary and everyday (*vivienda*), metaphor is what really catches hold of the "inner doing" (*fazienda*) of a character's mind, which Galdós sees as the essence of being.

93

Metaphor is generally defined as a figure of speech that contains an implicit comparison, in which a word or phrase for one thing is applied to another, either to illuminate a likeness by the use of a parallel structure or to reveal similarities by comparing different things with certain, unexpected likenesses. In *Fortunata and Jacinta* these likenesses, not immediately visible, constitute what is unusual in the ordinary, making up the "news" in Galdós's novel. The narrator takes up a bit of gossip and plays with the words, construing even the simplest of these as a pun or an image of *something*, a sign for hidden facts or feelings, concepts or values. Relying on Villalonga's news he appears not to stylize what is known or accepted as real, yet his use of metaphor is so basic and pervasive that figures of speech become an intrinsic part of mimesis, as opposed to embellishment, appearing to move in the text as animated pieces of life.

In the opening chapters, as the narrator tells of family alliances, facts cited in a casual manner become motifs that weave an almost tangible interrelatedness, shaped in a kind of analogical matrix – a central cluster of comparisons from which images spring. Narration gives rise to figures of thought and speech that *engender* a net of images. As we have seen, this net or *enredo*, embedded within the *enredadera* of Madrid's grapevine and proliferating among the spreading leaves and branches of the great family tree, denotes the ramifying lineage (linkage) that gives rise to plot. At the same time, *enredo*, "plot" and *enredadera*, "grapevine," overlap to specify the analogy between living a story and telling a life, thus developing in new ways the tension between history and fiction, between resemblances and differences that metaphor itself is empowered to maintain.

The narrator's use of analogy and metaphor establishes the remarkable coherence and complexity of *Fortunata and Jacinta*. It also appears to privilege the very notion of image, so that the concepts of comparison and dialectic, reiterated in figures of speech, appear to structure the story internally and offer, as Hafter says, unconscious illuminations that underscore the intricate mesh of form and matter (MH, 233).

Here metaphor's etymon – from *meta*, beyond, and *fora*,
carry (a verb related to the Latin *ferre*, with its past participle
latum) – becomes obliquely relevant to this basic, finely
worked interrelatedness of Galdós's novel. As a matrix of
images the family tree, for example, *takes* perception further,
beyond what we already know, and thus informs known things
with the notion of *latitude*, while presenting configurations
that keep reiterating the basic image of vines and leaves.
As proliferating *enredaderas* wind their way forward and
back, returning always to the trunk of the tree, and as various
motifs relate (telling, connecting), in the two-fold meaning
of that verb in Spanish and English, they create an alternating
movement through the text. These correlations make an
exceptionally dense yet expanding novelistic world, one in
which the etymon and the construct of metaphor appear to
relate to Galdós's theoretical equation, while analogy itself
reiterates the origin of a story-telling we find expressively
shaped as the family tree.

The branching connections of the family tree disclose how
apparently disparate, scattered things are bound by invisible
likenesses. In his fabric store Estupiñá's idle yardstick "flowers"
into Saint Joseph's venerable staff; close by, in her bedroom,
a button comes bounding toward Jacinta, "blinking" its mute
message of Juan's infidelity; next door, Moreno-Isla, thinking
of Jacinta, remembers the painting of Saint Joseph, staff and
Child in hand, that presided over his childhood. The "placid,"
dreamy yardstick ("vara"), identified with don *Plácido* and
with José, father of Jesus and patron saint of Estupiñá's
real-life counterpart, José Luengo, "branches out" to embrace
that button buried deep within the family tree. Its flowering
vine traces out a second "story" that runs counter to the
novelas of Juanito Santa Cruz, that principal (not principled)
character whom the narrator has imagined as an idle, inert
"clothes tree." In effect, wood of the Holy Cross *does not
flower* in marriage but only *deflowers* outside the home as
Santa Cruz doffs consorts according to fashion's whim and
drops lovers as dry leaves, discarding them as texts already
read.

The linkage of cloth and text motifs creates unexpected juxtapositions and a dual perspective that conveys the more subtle ironies of *Fortunata and Jacinta*. A button reveals how a man-child, that "hombre-niño" of Jacinta's dream, sires the son that both Estupiñá and Moreno also appear to *father*, as indicated by the allusions to the Biblical patriarch San José. The allusion appears almost as a prophecy, since stupid old Estupiñá, by occasioning the initial encounter between Juanito and Fortunata in the beginning and by smuggling the button-eyed baby to Jacinta in the end, brings about the substitution of the childish Juanito by that child. Now Estupiñá's beloved *Dauphin* ("*Delfín*") finds himself overtaken by the little "*Dauphin*" (*el Delfinito*), revealed to be none other than the "little egg dealer" ("*hueverito*") whom Jacinta had imagined into being on the honeymoon. Thus at the end Juanito Santa Cruz, a divine man-child at the center of the family and baptised by Estupiñá as the Dauphin, becomes effaced from the royal house by Fortunata's son. A new dynasty of egg sellers, as old as their Spanish origins in la Cava, replaces the old rule of a newly minted Frenchified prince, and a lost button becomes the baby Jacinta imagines she has conceived with Moreno, a man who is not her husband. Unexpected likenesses, buried deep in the text, confirm the initial adulterous connotation of that button in a new way, challenging Villalonga's old and "remote" news — "las noticias más remotas" — which started up the family history as chronicled in Part 1.

Ballester's remark after Fortunata's funeral amplifies the concept of news and interrelatedness still further. What is good and bad go walking around in one harness, he says ("Bienes y males andan siempre aparejados en la vida"), careful to give the notion of goodness and badness a plural identity. The wordplay on pairs (*pares*) yokes together (*aparejados*) family origins (the paired marriages), as well as beginning (Trujillo mules) and end (a "yoked" set of values). In this way, the dual notion of *res*, in Latin the etymon of *real*, in Spanish, *res*, meaning *mule*, which started up the two stories of married women, now appears to jump alive and kicking into the end of those stories, "pulling" fact and fiction forward as one "harnessed" figure. Thus Ballester's metaphor of yoked values encapsulates a theory of the good, bad and real that relates to Galdós's theoretical equation. It is an abstraction (*belleza*) that maintains a footing in a particular experience (*exactitud*), since Ballester invents the image as he speaks of his passion for Fortunata, his grief and relief at her death.

Metaphors of mind

Ballester's image of yoked values and of Fortunata's life already written as a "play or novel" are instances of Cervantine irony, a kind of interior duplication that shows how fictions work, what a novel is and what *novelas* do. All this occurs within the novel we read, and thus the images appear to offer their own epistemological theory, making the genre itself into a kind of metaphor. As characters talk and tell, the narrator construes their stories as "fruits" of the great family tree, noting those that "ripen" and expand – the mixed genre of "raw fruit" and "compote" that represents Fortunata's life story – as opposed to the rehashed "scripts" and "editions" that "shrink" to the "dry nut" of Juanito's thinking. The notion of tree and stories becomes linked to the question of value. In Juan's case, the foliage of the family tree functions as camouflage, as fiction, whereas the living stories of Maxi and Fortunata are *novelas* that grow like leaves on the tree.

The linkage specifies how the family tree appears to engender four major metaphors for the "inner doing" of consciousness: (1) the image of stories (*novelas*), meaning the mental, moral and imaginative aspects of making a novel; (2) *telas, trapos, tejidos* – all the variants of cloth, clothing and fashion; (3) *máquina*, the machinery and mechanisms of an industrialized, manufacturing economy; and (4) *moneda*, money, in newly minted coins and paper bills, displayed as a new determinant of social custom, with emphasis on the cash nexus – liquidity, distribution and consumption – buying and selling, lending and borrowing. For example, Ido approaches Jacinta with his *novela* of the false Pituso, Fortunata slips a feeling among the folds of her mind, Santa Cruz cranks up his brightly oiled, thinking machine, and doña Lupe experiences a *transacción*, as in her mind she negotiates an "economic" compromise with Maxi's passion.

These four metaphorical clusters establish what is specific in the relation between psychological effect and the aesthetic properties of images. They also relate images to one another, to other proliferating *enredaderas* of the family tree, making a whole of image and text, a knot of motifs. The knot controls the distance from which we view the story, permitting a speculative activity that adds to the imaginative substance of character. The knot also permits us to apprehend certain words as puns and ironic little jokes that continuously release bite-sized, story-telling energies into narration. In *Fortunata and Jacinta*, the narrator's special, ironic way of joking – *socarronería* – relies upon the punning of metaphor, as in the interpolated description of don Basilio Andrés de la Caña. Noting the man's "pumpkin-headed baldness" and "resemblance to Cavour," the narrator cocks an ear to joking conversations in a Madrid café; "The best business deal these days would be – bet you can't guess – to crack open Basilio's head, take out all that straw and sell it."

Texts as textiles, salvation bought by the Virgin's robe, imagination as *máquina* and an adopted child as a counterfeit coin – these images derive from the four major metaphors. The motifs lend substance to thought and behavior, representing mental, emotional and spiritual phenomena as characters and events in themselves, replete with story-telling energies, *vida novelable*. As characters think, feel and imagine, the analogies lend a pictorial sense, dramatically close up, of gesturing hands, of eyes and ears and of mouths, bright and moist and breathing. Even the simplest utterance participates in an entwined configuration, as natural as the root, branch and leaf of the great family tree, as consequential as the time-honored correlation, emphasized in Spanish, between discourse, story-telling and spinning yarns (*discurrir/hilar*).

This correlation binds together the sense of social contexts and their bearing on the intimacy of private thinking. At the beginning, the manufacture of textiles, origin of story and text, produces two competing items of clothing. Each depicts national consciousness, a kind of metaphor of mind. The narrator takes time to unfold the great Manila shawl, those popular, legendary *mantones de Manila*, and compares them to *abrigos confeccionados*, "cooked-up" clothing imported from Paris. Somber, buttoned-down coats as opposed to brightly colored, unfurling shawls become *textual* signs for mental modes of behavior. The *mantón* pictures a native, quintessentially Spanish, disposition of the spirit, overcome and overlaid by the acquired tastes and habits manufactured by the "invasion" of fashions from France. The *mantón* unfurls as a poem, flower-splashed and fresh (*poema salpicado de flores*), innocent as a child, expressive of Fortunata's natural, "primitive" ways. Conversely, the ready-made, manufactured coats, frowning and inert, stand for the "covered" actions and tightly "buttoned" lips of the treacherous Aurora Fenelón, who speaks French and counts coins in francs. The double meaning of *contar* – counting and telling – crosses with the notion of French and frank/ness, turning confidentiality into betrayal. Another ironic point is scored in Part 4 as the franc-counting Aurora fences in wordplay with Fortunata, all the while pinning patterns to cloth, pricking pins between pursed lips, jabbing points into the dress front of her ample, spongy (*fofa*) bosom.

The dialogue between Fortunata and Aurora shows how the cloth trade, a fact of mass culture, relates metaphorically to other mass phenomena – *novelas*, published serially, and *dramas*, in loose-leaf formats costing less than a penny. Paper patterns on cloth become pinned, as it were, to the notion of the printed page, as both women fabricate stories, one telling the truth, the other intending to betray. In effect, *novelas* appear to underlie perception as both the narrator and the characters become "readers." Individual lives are seen as texts to be read and deciphered in *Fortunata and Jacinta*: Barbarita sees in that "trifling page" of her son's youth an amorous escapade or two; Jacinta wants to pry into "certain little pages" of her husband's past, and as for Juanito, pushed and pulled by volatile appetites, women are simply "texts" to be read, re-read and discarded periodically, like the daily paper. The narrator himself displays story-telling as a volitional act of "reading" and "writing" as he copies and edits, snipping off one thread ("hebra") to splice another, and he takes care to point to his reporting of events and to his jurisdiction only over words (JK, 286).

Novelas start up a self-consciously novelistic world. In Part 1, Juanito Santa Cruz climbs the stair to visit Estupiñá – here is the place, the narrator says, to talk about that visit, for if Juanito had not stepped into la Cava, "this novel would not have been written." Another novel, certainly, "since people always carry stories about them, but not this one," not this particular fiction that has turned into something historical, something real. Later Ido's interpolated *novela* asserts by comparison the veracity of the narrator's own story, while, as Kronik notes, such interpolated stories hint "that in a fiction-within-a-fiction *all* is fiction" (JK, 289).

Villalonga's "new narrative"

At the close of Part 1, Galdós creates a scene that plays with the literary idea of a mixed genre in a particularly clever way. It introduces the mischief of a text that appears to contain itself, while illustrating the dense and branching interrelatedness of *Fortunata and Jacinta*. The scene presents an adroitly "novelistic" mix of public and private events, relating these to certain traits of national and individual character, and projects a dramatic image of the "inner doing" that takes place between interrelating minds. As the scene evolves, the narrator's own account begins to approach in style and substance the notion of a "play or novel" advocated by Ballester and Ponce – in retrospect a genre that appears to coincide in part with the novel we read.

The title of this closing chapter, "An End that Turns Out to be a Beginning," also hints at the way an interpolated *novela* can overturn history, for, as the scene takes place, parallels between public and private life combine to shape a *novela* visually on the page. This novelistic shape, appearing

as a two-tiered dialogue which, of course, the characters themselves cannot see, conveys some unexpected insights into their
psychology and to the times. The shape also shows Galdós's
theoretical equation at work, as the representation of historical
fact (*exactitud*) combines with a new aesthetic form (*belleza*)
to tell the news: here upon the page is a *novela-noticia* or
"new narrative" that appears to propel the plot forward as
it places that plot within an ironic, evaluative perspective.

The episode stages a conversation between the corrupt
politician, Jacinto María Villalonga, who is responsible for
those very first *noticias*, and Juanito Santa Cruz, titular
personage of Part 1. The conversation, cast as a little dramatic
scene, illustrates to perfection the connections of those four
governing metaphors of mind – *novelas*, machinery, money
and the manufacture of cloth. In this way, precisely at the end
of Part 1, that familiar knot of motifs, now metonymic in
function, works retrospectively to amplify and qualify those
metaphors of mind that had characterized Juanito Santa Cruz
as titular prince of the beginning of the book. We find, then,
at the close of Part 1, a scene that dramatizes beginnings
and endings as Villalonga presents himself at the door of the
Santa Cruz house. He has come with more than one story to
tell and as Jacinta, his reluctant *tocaya* ("name-mate"), ushers
him into the hall, don Jacinto hastens on to the bedroom where
his *amigote*, Juan, is dressing. Time is of the essence, for a
story – a *noticia* – like this one will not wait:

– Chico, ¿no sabes … la noticia que te traigo? … ¡Si supieras a
quién he visto! ¿Nos oirá tu mujer?
– No, hombre, pierde cuidado – replicó Juan, poniéndose los
botones de la pechera –. Claréate pronto.
– Pues yo he visto a quien menos puedes figurarte … Está aquí.
– ¿Quién?
– Fortunata … Pero no tienes idea de su transformación. ¡Vaya
un cambiazo! Está guapísima, elegantísima. Chico, me quedé
turulato cuando la vi.   (431–32)

"You simply can't imagine, my lad … the news I've got! If you
only knew whom I've seen! Can your wife hear us?"
"No, don't worry" – replied Juan, setting studs in his shirt front.
"Come out with it, fast."

"Well, I've seen someone you'd least expect ... She's here."
"Who?"
"Fortunata. But you've no idea how she's changed. What a
transformation! She looks fabulous, just stunning. Man, my jaw
almost dropped when I saw her."

The date is 6 January 1874, *el día de Reyes* (Three Kings'
Day, that is, Twelfth Night), a date that represents a "stitch"
taken in the overall pattern which rules the narrative point
of view with regard to the social and political prominence of
Don Baldomero I and II and the princely privileges of *el
Delfín*. The date also foretells an important political event:
the restoration of the Bourbon monarchy the following year.
Already the monarchy metaphor connects, and on Three
Kings' Day Villalonga, bearing the gift of a startling *noticia*,
appears in his tripartite role as *amigo, amigote* and *amante*.
Closest to Juan, he also enjoys access to the aristocratic
colonel don Evaristo Feijoo, as well as to Juan Pablo Rubín,
eldest nephew in doña Lupe's household, and even exchanges a
patronizing word or two with the wretched Villaamil. Villaamil's
nickname *Ramsés II* makes its own mockery of the hopes
that the monarchy, soon to be restored in the person of the
boyish king Alfonso XII, holds out to the multitudes of urban
poor (*Villa-mil*). Villalonga is also a smug, uppvr-class gentleman (*señorito satisfecho*), a lover of courtesans like Antoñita,
who decorates dinner plates with her palette much as don
Vicente López, favored by high society, had painted the glossy
portrait of Don Baldomero I (*el grande*), admired first-hand
by the narrator himself. And while slumming with Santa Cruz,
Villalonga has made the acquaintance of simpler women of
the people, like Fortunata and Mauricia *la Dura*, who, when
in need of money, frequent a popular brothel.

In sum, Villalonga on Three Kings' Day relates both to
the narrator and to representatives of the three social classes.
He appears to surface everywhere like a bad penny, extending
himself through the city (*Villa-longa*) to link and exchange
public and private affairs, marriage and money, politics and
story-telling, introducing public events into private scenes
arranged to exclude them. And here, at the close of Part 1

as in the opening sentence, Villalonga appears as a gossiper (*enrededor*), marking the origin of the novel's plot (*enredo*) and its development in dialogue, here broken by slips of the tongue that punctuate his stuttering, stumbling rendition of the urgent news. His "new narrative" is in fact only another chapter in the old *novela* that Juanito carries within himself. It is a bit of news, *noticia*, which in conjunction with other bits "builds" the metaphor *vida-novela* into a veritable house of fiction, a genre on the rise in 1874 as the chief literary expression of a capitalist economy. In Old Madrid this economy was based on the manufacture of cloth, and Juan, it will be noted, is in the act of dressing, setting his studs.

As the scene evolves we find that Villalonga has arrived not with one but with two stories to tell: the account of a political upset — General Manuel Pavía's coup — which he exploits as a visible counterpart to another upset — the sudden appearance of Fortunata in a café. In effect, responding to Jacinta's interruptions, he tells a two-part story, which appears on the page as a two-tiered structure: Fortunata as protagonist occupies the "lower" half, while Villalonga and his political party, surreptitiously pitted against the orator Salmerón, occupy the upper "story" of parliamentary debate. The paired stories ramify the monarchy metaphor, each depicting, at least momentarily, the overthrow of a reigning institution. Pavía's coup forces the dissolution of the republican government, toppling the presidency of Castelar, while Villalonga's own fabulous picture ("visión inverosímil") of Fortunata, gowned in blue velvet, overturns the supposedly monogamous, "monarchical" marriage of *el Delfín* and *la Delfina* — the young Santa Cruz couple.

Pavía's coup, however, so ably abetted by Villalonga who prides himself on being in the know, unintentionally precipitates a narrative structure that also overturns our perception of Villalonga's capacities *qua* story-teller and politician. Two supposedly factual bits of news are juxtaposed, one concerning the "top," the other the "bottom." Villalonga presents Salmerón's defeat in Parliament as a way to dissemble the real news of having seen Fortunata in a café. But the contemporary public event appears to change places with the private episode. The report of the orator's speech becomes an improvised *novela*, whereas Fortunata's appearance in a café takes on urgent attributes of the real, of the "res," meaning the "wild game" that Santa Cruz soon will pursue throughout Old Madrid. Jacinta's unexpected entries into the room, interrupting the conversation, force Villalonga to jump nimbly from one account to the other:

> ¡Pero si habías de verla tú! ... Yo, te confieso, estaba pasmado, absorto, embebe ...,
> ¡Ay, Dios mío! entró Jacinta y Villalonga tuvo que dar un quiebro violentísimo ...
> – Te digo que estaba embebecido. El discurso de Salmerón fue admirable ... pero lo más admirable ... Aún me parece que estoy viendo aquella cara de hijo de desierto, y aquel movimiento horizontal de los ojos y la gallardía de los gestos. (434)

> "But you simply have to see her for yourself! ... As for me, I admit: I was stunned, dazzled, struck ..."
> Oh, good grief! Jacinta came in and Villalonga spun on his heel to change the subject ...
> "I tell you, I was struck dumb! Salmerón's speech was amazing, really amazing ... I can still see that face, that 'prophet of the desert' look, the sideways slant of his eyes and the gallantry of his gestures."

Two modes of discourse – confession ("Yo, te confieso") and solemn statement ("Te digo") point up the difference between the two accounts, yet the two-tiered structure appears to match the bits of news: one reflects the other; one is as fictional as the other. Fortunata is hardly that Parisian prostitute – Joaquín Pez catches sight of her the next day entering a pawn shop – and Salmerón's speech is a flamboyant fake. Villalonga, behind the scenes, recounts that fakery, mocking the orator's melodramatic gestures. But what he does not see is how his own manner of telling, staged as a dramatic scene and acted out in histrionic gestures, appears constructed on the page as a two-tiered, architectonic conceit, "built" into upper and lower "stories." In effect, Villalonga's story mimics Salmerón's speech. Both are politicians; both present the wild-eyed look of a prophet born of the desert, both take recourse to grand rhetoric, posturing "gallantly," glancing significantly. It is this resemblance that frames the unknowing Villalonga, even as he springs the trap of his party's conspiracy on the unsuspecting Salmerón, even as he frames the news of Fortunata's appearance under the cover of a political coup.

Later, over coffee and liqueur, Villalonga gives yet another rendition of Pavía's coup, which the narrator compares to ripened grapes left at the bottom of a fruit basket. The image denotes the tastiness of gossipy news, recalls the grapevine of the family tree and alludes to appetites piqued as Fortunata is described. Villalonga's two-tiered news ite.n has "depth," and like that fruit basket it contains appetizing morsels: the young woman, gowned in luscious blue velvet, "está de rechupete" – "she's 'finger-lickin' good'", Villalonga exclaims. The word *chupete* refers to a nipple or baby's pacifier, while the prefix *re*, an intensifier, suggests the emphatic gesture of kissing one's fingertips, waving an arm. Villalonga describes how the low-cut gown "presents" her breasts as perfectly "exploded" ("en perfecta *explotación*!"), the verb *explotar* meaning also to "exploit," and her plump, tiny earlobes pierced by turquoise drops invite kisses, mouthing bites – "Oh what divine little ears! You could've gobbled them right up!" he pants, whispering to Juan. The pierced earlobes particularly obsess Juan's imagination because they denote penetration and a cultivated sexuality. Thus the habitual, half-conscious act of setting dress studs in his shirt front becomes an oblique allusion to desires already "set" in the psyche of this philandering husband who in three brief years of marriage has had at least six affairs.

The entwined connections of these images, which appear as part of a manufactured account about cloth cut to fashion (a blue velvet gown, a starched and studded white shirt front), set in an erotic context of financial transactions (prostitution) and public and private exchanges (monarchy restored and monogamy overturned), display the four governing metaphors (*novelas, máquina, moneda, tela*). These specify the differences between Fortunata and Jacinta, yet, at the same time, equate them still further, since an appetite for novelties motivates

Juan's attentions to his wife and his mistress alike. With
Jacinta, as with Fortunata, he seeks to taste pure virtue, as
if it were a ripe fruit: "purity itself pricks the appetite," says
the narrator, and thus Jacinta appeals periodically to Juan
"as if she were someone else's wife." Juan is unfaithful even
to his wife's own identity and role *qua* Jacinta.

The analogies call attention to yet another aspect of Villalonga's news, in that he "smuggles" his depiction of a transformed Fortunata under the "cloak" of that recounted event
of the Pavía coup. The metaphorical action of smuggling
obliquely links this scene to the birth of Fortunata's child
and the gift of that child to Jacinta. In effect, the newborn child
becomes precious contraband, "smuggled" under Estupiñá's
cloak down the stone staircase, *from one "story" to another*,
just as Villalonga had "smuggled" the news of Fortunata
down from one story-telling level to another. Moreover,
Villalonga's two "stories," "built" into an "edifice," acquire
the double function of edification and evasion: they cover
and dis-cover at the same time. As recipient of the dual *noticia*,
Juan's attention inhabits the "lower" story. Leaning forward,
bending down to glean information and receive instruction,
he seeks to be edified, pressing for details with a piqued
interest ("picado de curiosidad"). As he *sets his studs* he
fabricates in collusion with Villalonga that fictional upper
"story," *set out* for the outsider, Jacinta. She nonetheless
remains related to Fortunata as she presses a *shell-pink ear*
("orejita sonrosada") to the keyhole in order to capture
something of those delectable, *jeweled ear lobes* of her rival,
in a frustrated effort to tie together the *ends* of a story about
to *begin*.

And in a still more oblique, structural way, the chapter
title that introduces Villalonga into the Santa Cruz house
sketches out still another kind of spatial architectonic figuring.
The title "sits atop," as it were, a statement of resolution,
an enacted ending, of a patriarchal power recognized and
accepted and of acquiescence of one inferior to her superiors.
Don Baldomero decrees that the child adopted by Jacinta
must be interned in Guillermina's orphanage. This is ostensibly

the end that the title reverses into a beginning. But the connection between title and initial statement hints at a further paradox: it suggests how a known and accepted decorum might turn into something else. For if ends become beginnings, specifying an unstable literary context, then a patriarchal government, both in family and nation, is likely also to undergo reversal, with power dethroned and stability undermined from below.

This, of course, is what occurs in Villalonga's stories of the political coup and Fortunata: Pavía overturns the current regime and Fortunata, pressing from "lower" social strata, upsets a marriage, supplanting monogamy with the free-living ways of "las cantonalas" − Jacinta's term for wanton women whose disrespect for matrimonial vows are compared, in her mind, to the cantons in Cartagena and Murcia that were rebelling against the Government at the time. Thus by virtue of the match between chapter title and interpolated story, the resultant misalliance struck between title and first sentence points forward and back to foretell larger misalliances and wider gaps. Such gaps expand to encompass the end and beginning of the novel itself, for the personal entitlement of the very first chapter, counterpoised to the absence of entitlement in the last, draws a circle around empty spaces with regard to Juanito Santa Cruz, *el del fin* ("Delfín"). When Juanito's exit becomes a pun on endings (*fin* of *el del-fín*), the *novela* of vanity turns into a joke.

Thus the one-word title of the novel's last chapter − "Final" − appears retrospectively as an abbreviation, an amputation, of the previous title that closes Part 1. This meaning, stemming from the word play "Final" in both titles, ironically reflects the title of the opening chapter of the novel, marking the discrepancy between the fully named beginning and the end which has no proper name at all. Despite what don Baldomero decrees, family entitlements come round to nothing and family resemblances work to bring about an *end* to likenesses. *El Del-fín* exits as a blank on the page, effaced by ends reversed into beginnings and "cuckolded" by Jacinta's own *novela*, in which Moreno-Isla supplants him as lover, husband and father of *el Delfinito*.

The realism of *Fortunata and Jacinta*

The effect of Villalonga's "storied" accounts, "built" upon the page as an "edifice," and the narrator's depiction of Juan's mind as a "house of fiction" endow imagination with physical and spatial attributes. The four major metaphors (*novela, tela, máquina, moneda*) that depict the collective mind share a common spatial topography, in which depth articulated by layers cause *nivelar* (level) and *novelar* (novel-making) to become almost interchangeable terms (JK, 275). The various *novelas* are interwoven; *manufactured cloth* both covers (satin walls, velvet gown) and conceals (coats, curtains); *money* buys the appearance of virtue and of a thriving, industrious spirit. A perception of this basic hypocrisy leads Fortunata to understand the division between public life and private life, and to see in everyday existence the image of a clock – the face visible, the mechanism hidden. Everywhere people strain to put on a proper face – " 'live peacefully on the inside and keep up a decent front' " admonishes Feijoo.

The clock image specifies how public and private minds assume a tangible expression. What is most elusive often becomes most concrete, as when the narrator imagines sorrow in "sedimentary layers," depicts manic thinking by alluding to ideas that roll about like beads of mercury or represents coarse thinking as ideas that bristle, black and hairy, upon the "balconies" of nose and ear. When reflecting on the nuns' educative efforts to reform Fortunata, he also distinguishes between a knowledge of surfaces and deeper structures. He speaks of a darker "realm" of passion where unformed feelings live and move about, acting as agents of change. Metaphors substantiate invisible thoughts and feelings, which thereby appear real, located in time and space, and subject to motion.

The notion of tangible minds specifies a kind of pre-Freudian psychoanalytic method. Story-telling becomes a strategy of associative thinking which aims at deciphering the past from signs in the present. On the honeymoon Jacinta hears a seller's cry "bocas de la Isla" and thinks of Fortunata. Why in the world would "bocas de la Isla" bring Fortunata to mind? asks the narrator — "Fresh anchovies from Cádiz" have absolutely nothing to do with her. But as a popular figure of speech, "bocas de la Isla," ostensibly referring to the mouth ("boca") of Cadiz harbor, have everything to do with Fortunata's story. Mouth and lips ("bocas"), fresh and inviting, have already prompted kisses and will incite mouthing bites, as Villalonga's account confirms at the close of Part 1. "Isla" ("island") prefigures her isolation and the untold story of her affinity in spirit to the alienated Moreno-Isla.

The hidden logic of associative thinking conveys a sense of intelligibility at the base of those criss-crossing stories of *Fortunata and Jacinta*. As the narrator interprets changing love triangles and the course of Maxi's madness, he builds a coherent, if not entirely systematic, psychoanalytic account of action and passion. He accentuates the mechanical in Santa Cruz, the emotional in Fortunata and Jacinta and the imaginative in Maxi, highlighting a mix of intellect and passion in Mauricia. In speaking of her mind as "lit like a lantern" he shows how she herself invents and interprets the lantern image. However demented, then, Mauricia understands her own mind, as does doña Lupe, who is aware of her own bossiness and volcanic temper, and Fortunata likewise becomes increasingly reflective, commenting upon her own story, interpreting inflections of speech and the most insignificant gestures. Ballester sees the craziness of love even as he lives it, and Maxi, quite mad, knows he is going to an insane asylum.

What is most subjective and fantastic appears associated with the logic and intelligibility of what is most physically and quantifiably real. In *Fortunata and Jacinta* story-telling itself, entwined in metaphor, executes a particularly subtle refinement of this relation between what is rational and real and what is imagined. Often Galdós places narration at borderline vantage points — doorways, curtains, transoms, balconies and windows — in order to direct attention to where information is communicated and received. In this way certain figures of speech, occurring at points of intersection between minds, appear to mimic a kind of physical or chemical process. When telling the story of the Rubín family, for example, the narrator uses metaphors that allude specifically to the kinesthesia of "gas-surface" interactions, similar to those that take place in cloud formation, corrosion and respiration. We recall the puffery of those gubernatorial pretensions of doña Lupe *la ministra* alias *la baronesa de Rothschild*; the gusts of ambition that blow two or three times a day through Juan Pablo's empty brain or the gaseous eruptions of the priest Nicolás. In the Rubín household, inflation − airy speculation spun by inflated egos in an inflated, unstable bourgeois economy − assumes progressively degraded forms. "Gaseous highs" reverse into moral "lows" as we descend from the magisterial airs of doña Lupe to those "frothing egg whites" of Juan Pablo's scarce ideas, "beaten" into fullness within that place of friction between narrator and character, finally to receive, full in the face, a "cubic meter of gas" belched by a prideful cleric with a mind full of hot air. Metaphors describe these "chemical" transformations − how ideas suddenly "vaporize," "bulge" or "explode," how consciousness "dissolves" or "liquifies," how remorse or sorrow "solidifies," or "sticks," like a stone in the throat. In effect, story-telling, like the chemistry of the real world, takes place at interfaces and edges, where the "inner doing" of consciousness or oblivion arises, where truths are told or lies fabricated, and where even a sum of money, *colocado* − that is *set* upon the *edge* of new trans-actions − changes into *guano*, fertilizer. Once again the comparison between minds and money is apt: minds taken to extremes, to the edge of what is commonly known (*vivienda*), expand, grow and change (*fazienda*), like Fortunata's, Jacinta's and Maxi's. Encapsulated minds like Juanito's stay put, and like money, when hoarded, grow corrupt.

In effect, Galdós uses metaphor to resolve the apparent conflict between objective and subjective modes in a realist novel. Figurative speech not only amplifies the notion of what is real; it also persuades us of the truthfulness of the represen-tation by grounding images in physical and chemical processes (friction, boiling points), nature (animals, trees), and social and economic phenomena of the times (cloth, money). The depiction of the consistency as well as the topography of matter, and the recognition of parallel distinctions in the "physi-ology" of the mind ("layers," "inner recesses," "skeletons," outer "shells" or "skins") also directs us to essential questions – what the mind is, how we know what it is, what effects one mind has on another, how to understand those effects and whether or not it makes a difference. Galdós's use of metaphor appears to posit the fact, at least from the outset, that story-telling minds and their relations can be known, that there are *down there* or *in there* discernible truths to be "fathomed," "fished up" and eventually "caught" in the "nets" of that enormous *enredadera*. To make this point the narrator uses transitional tags that refer to "truth," "reality" or "hard money" – money, after all, is gospel truth in a society founded on economic laws as immutable as gravity. The assumption is that an "immense realm of the passions" does exist; that minds, tangible and corporeal like "spiritual skeletons," also exist and are predictable, passing through and enduring over time; lastly, that such realms can be and ought to be explored. Novelists, like scientists or psychoanalysts, may not rest content with a technique of surfaces, like the timorous nuns of Las Micaelas.

Thus Galdós's use of metaphor as both an agent of moral reasoning and of novelistic invention appears to affirm the idea that the effect of authenticity or truthfulness is the primary aspect of what is real in the contemporary social novel. No longer is the conflict between ideology and mimesis relevant, as in earlier debates about so-called "thesis" novels like *Doña Perfecta* (1876) or *Gloria* (1877). In *Fortunata and Jacinta*, truthful realization and the question of morality cannot be separated, since the nature of truth, whether imagi-native or scientific, is here made to rest upon the coherence of a particular metaphorical system and not upon a perception of "objective" truth. The "combination," as Ballester says, not only instructs but is therapeutic. On the one hand, the depiction of Old Madrid appears to be objective, a faithful mirror of the times, a social world founded upon fixed, economic laws. But on the other hand money is liquid and moves into metaphor as the narrator construes the family tree as an analogical matrix, making of metaphor itself both an agent of interrelatedness and the artistic expression of relations – running vines ("enredaderas") of cloth, commerce, *cuento*. Stories (*cuentos, novelas*), spun as plots (*enredos*) within tangled grapevines (*enredaderas*) among bits of news ("noticias"), call attention to the novel as a subjective process of thinking and imagining, emphasizing the narrative structure of fictions-within-a-fiction. This composite, oblique structure enjoins us to perceive the various *novelas* and to evaluate one *novela* in terms of another. As Ballester says, good things and bad things, yoked together, walk around in one harness.

At the beginning of *Fortunata and Jacinta* Juanito offered his own theory about *novelas*. He compared them to real and imagined cutlets and preferred to taste one himself rather than hear about it. Yet the story we read begins with Juanito's own *novela*, and from beginning to end idle *señoritos* are fed stories (*chuletas*) occasioned by plebian girls (*chulitas*) of Old Madrid. Despite his stated preference for the real thing, Santa Cruz knows how to turn pork chops into spiritual stuff ('espiritualizar las cosas materiales") – he keeps inventing *novelas* as he talks to his reflection in the mirror or retells Fortunata's story to Jacinta or Jacinta's story to Fortunata.

Moreover, the texts of Santa Cruz's *novelas* display the four basic metaphors, reiterating stylistically his social importance and centrality. But the metaphors appear in debased, material-istic forms, and as *novelas*, imagined mechanically, they now appear as staged stories or scripts fatigued with use. There is the sense, in his narrative "prestidigitations," that the genre itself has been exchanged for other amusements – theater, opera, circus and carnival. Manufactured cloth, used to dress up ideas, now becomes a substitute for thought itself, and money takes behavior to the gaming table. The metaphors depict Santa Cruz's mind as a stratified thing, honeycombed with "crevices" and "caverns," a hidden "container" of secrets that resists "fathoming." Juan's *novelas*, like Villalonga's new narrative, build layer upon layer a kind of "architecture" of deceit and self-deception, reflected in the way images become substantiated as the real thing.

Ultimately, however, the spacial topography of these novelistic inventions corrupts the inventor himself. When telling
about Juan's reactions on the honeymoon the narrator notes
how any spontaneous feelings lie discarded at the bottom of
the man's soul "like pieces of a gaudy costume" left piled
in a "corner" by a person "who used to be an actor," and
then only an "amateur." The image specifies those levels
that confound reasoning, for Santa Cruz cannot know his
own mind and therefore cannot reflect. Reflection, though,
relates only to mirror images, play-acting and punning, and
the narrator suggests the double meaning of *reflection* in
words like *reflexivo*, *reflejo*, *reflexionar*, which reiterate the
narcissistic *self-sameness* of the reflexive construction. In
that construction two or more referents match each other
in a convergence of sound and shape that actually signals
divergence, discrepancy. Thus the reflections of this "reflexive
man" point not to thought but to the absence of thought
as he "bends back" to rely upon comedies and melodrama,
old scripts written by his mother and upon current fashion.
Talking to his image in the mirror, Santa Cruz asserts, "we're
really *something*," while the narrator's use of the reflexive
shows he is nothing.

Conversely, those *novelas* imagined by Jacinta and Moreno,
Fortunata and Maxi, are alive, light, ascendant; they breathe.
Allusions to air, blowing or buffeting about characterize
the "inner doing" of their image-making minds. Fortunata
fluffs feathers, the shawl unfurls and her mind turns in the
wind as a weathervane. Maxi gauges his love by the spinning
disk of the pump outside Las Micaelas. Moreno's "dove-ideas"
flock through skies and Jacinta's "whirlwind of thoughts"
recasts him as the father of the child. A dying, half-literate,
working-class girl affirms that she is an angel and we know
that is true. Something angelic has agitated her spirit from
the beginning. As Maxi's friend Olmedo says, there is something
angelic about her ("Tiene un ángel"), and, returning from
her funeral, both Maxi and Ballester affirm her angelic grace.
Jacinta imagines she and Moreno are parents of the child
and their relationship is of far more value than her marriage

to Juan. Maxi lives in the stars, next to mules in a mudhole ("muladar"). Yet Fortunata and Moreno are dead, Jacinta only adopts the child and Maxi goes mad. These facts put to question the efficacy or the value of their *novelas* in comparison to Juan's.

The age-old metaphor of life as a story (*novela*) thus appears to "solidify" in Galdós's text as a literary and moral problem. It appears to question itself *qua* image, as when Santa Cruz expounds his philosophy of life as an imagined or tasted pork chop and talks to his reflection in the mirror. Here Galdós hints at a self-referential process that establishes comparison and contrast as fundamental to the real, and directs us to larger questions about value. In effect, whenever something is substituted for something else, the question of rightness or wrongness emerges, and on occasion substitution itself becomes suspect. One example is a conversation in church between Barbarita and Estupiñá: she tells the rosary, he babbles news of bargains in the market place. Questions and responses, crossing on the page, appear to *swap* religion for shopping, and the dialogue turns into a "scenic" metaphor that discloses the questionable nature of Barbarita's religious vocation.

When Juan exchanges one "pork chop" for another or Guillermina labors to provide the child with a surrogate mother, substitution, conveyed by metaphor, calls attention to comparison and to the likeness, carried in the etymon, between comparing (*comparare*) and buying (*comprar*). Now we begin to suspect certain metaphor-making minds as particularly expressive of the limitations of social class, and, whenever they appear to shop around for the right words, they resemble "products" of a manufacturing economy. Juan relies on clichés that reify thinking and feeling, whereas his use of formulaic speech reveals a tendency toward categorical or socially prejudicial ways of thinking. The priest Nicolás, who keeps stating opinions as "things" ("esto es la cosa"), is comically at fault, but on occasion Guillermina also speaks patronizingly of Fortunata's spirit as a "thing" ("esto es cosa"). Both religious workers stay stuck in the *res* of received social codes. Even the dictatorial doña Lupe employs a cliché

that suggests more flexibility: things "stretch out" in words
("en toda la extensión de la palabra") to admit the notion of
"transaction" – of change, not exchange, and of relative,
not absolute, truths.

Not surprisingly, Galdós associates Fortunata with plain
speech and truth-telling. The essence of her being is anti-
thetical to metaphor – why say something when it is something
else, she thinks. The narrator agrees, though at first he assists
thought, explicating Fortunata's garbled speech to give the
illusion that hers is a natural style. Her speech "leafs out"
(*reverdecer*) on the tongue or gives way to inarticulate sounds
of pure feeling. Her thinking originates in the senses, primarily
touch, hence the emphasis on hands, on sensual perception
and, as she responds to feelings, on reflective habits of mind.
Her "pícara idea" surges from deepest strata, "from within
herself" as she contemplates what she thinks, occasionally
taking the initiative, as when she compares her mind to a
weathervane. Here is an instructive paradox: although the
narrator uses metaphors sparingly with Fortunata, the "inner
doing" of her consciousness is the most effervescent in the
novel. In this way Fortunata, born fortuitously from an egg,
appears to be the most natural character in Galdós's novel.

Conversely, Maxi's thinking starts evolving through images.
For him, reality is only a matter of names, and his mind
keeps reinventing the world, substituting one thing for another,
reversing, as he says, night into day. If dreaming and waking
are states of mind, he reasons, why is one thing more real
than another? This transformative naming astonishes the
narrator, who, as in the case of Mauricia, relies on metaphor
as he labors to map Maxi's manic but often inspired thinking.
The building blocks of physics (fission, boiling points, clock-
springs) appear to ground images in the verifiably real, but
Maxi's finger-snapping mind dances away, and, when pursued,
he is a "res" like Fortunata – "wild game that slips away"
("la res que no cae"). From this Galdós's bourgeois narrator
learns that imagination and madness are not quantifiable,
fixed states, but are functions, capable of change. Thus Maxi,
like don Quijote, remains to the end what Cervantes calls an

"intermixed lunatic, full of lucid intervals" (AC, 77). Quite mad, he nonetheless comes to know himself, to decipher his love and to recognize Fortunata as both human and angelic. He knows the insane asylum for what it really is, while at the same time he lives, as he says, "in the stars." In this sense Maxi himself *becomes* an image; he incarnates Galdós's theoretical equation by achieving a "perfect point of balance" between fact (asylum) and beauty (stars). Maxi, richest in spirit, manifests what is real in the most ambivalent way in Galdós's novel.

The depiction of Santa Cruz's thinking, which shows how dialectic has congealed into paradox, offers another paradoxical turn when we consider that this mind, compared in its limitations to a "shrunken nut," nonetheless constitutes for the narrator a particularly rich repository of metaphor. A worldling, surfeited with pleasures and convinced of his own "realist" views, Juanito is not introspective, nor is he conscious of any "inner doing" in himself or in others. Only clichés − half-dead metaphors − lace his discourse. But the narrator appears to quarry his mind, executing brilliantly original figures of speech − Juanito "dresses up" thought, "ironing the collars of language," or "plays with the dice-cups of reason." Why does a banal, contractive mind appear to expand as a rich source for metaphor? Richness betokens the narrator's obsession with Santa Cruz, whose thinking presents a clear and present danger to the social body. Whatever passes through Juanito's mind turns into a trickster's fiction (*triquiñuelas*). Things are not what they seem; appearances usurp what is real, and naming acquires a taxonomic function, as this prince specifies in a professorial manner the proprieties of social decorum. Thus Juanito corrects word usage, reproves grammar and dictates to Jacinta and Fortunata what a woman's role should be in society.

The very banality of his views and his childish nature assure the survival of such reasoning in Restoration society, where women applaud King Alfonso XII because he is hardly more than a child. Childishness in women and old men like Barbarita and Estupiñá appears harmless enough; their little charades in the marketplace, on the look-out for "pure sensations," attest merely to boredom. Nor does childishness in a handicapped man like Maxi pose a threat. But infantile appetites in grown men of power are the root of wrongdoing in *Fortunata and Jacinta*. The problem originates in Madrid households where a male child rules as king. Unlike behaviors taken to extremes, like Mauricia's rampages, Guillermina's desire for sacrifice, Maxi's crazed strivings or Ballester's exalted love, childishness in grown men persists in the guise of equilibrium, benevolence or charm. The narrator is determined to find out this childishness in grown men, whose power and privilege cause self-serving views to appear just and reasonable. So he takes recourse to Galdós's theoretical equation, applying one kind of balance to expose the injurious disorder of another. Particularly, he selects figures of speech that reveal faulty thinking, using metaphor to give notice where it counts, to members of the household, just as Villalonga had done with his *noticia-novela* – news like grapes left at the bottom of the basket.

Metaphor instructs. Metaphor is real. It has become an instrument of knowledge that teases out the unknown, forming the underlying paradoxes of thinking and feeling that animate the entwined stories of *Fortunata and Jacinta*. As these stories unfold, then, we find that metaphor displays a mimetic function, tracing out and qualifying the thinking process itself. It appears that Galdós's novel is not just *there* but continues to happen as we read, and to happen in a new way each time, thereby becoming most natural when it appears most contrived. Particularly in the episode of Villalonga's "new narrative," the expanding and contracting analogies link thinking and feeling, and make the *novelas* of Salmerón and Villalonga, and of Villalonga and Juanito, one, while at the same time revealing ironic discrepancies. As a result, Galdós's metaphorical system appears to have selected the imagining mind as the best diagnostic tool for conducting a study of itself, and of the four-part novel as a landmark in the realist tradition that such a system has ushered into being.

Galdós's genius lies precisely in his ability to make the

artistically complex appear artless and available. Novel-writing appears as natural as breathing, as easy as drinking a glass of water. Valle-Inclán's disparaging remark that all in a Galdós novel is as plain as a plate of beans fails to recognize the real news that this novel contains. In *Fortunata and Jacinta*, Galdós's masterpiece, the ordinary and obvious become problematic, and, as little Maxi shows, what is ordinarily real always remains innocent of what it carries to the stars.

Guide to further reading

Editions, translations, mss.

P. Ortiz Armengol's annotated edition of *Fortunata and Jacinta* (1979), commissioned to commemorate the centenary of the publishing house Hernando (Madrid), contains genealogies, illustrations and maps of Old Madrid. A revised version of the notes, *Apuntaciones para Fortunata y Jacinta* (Madrid, 1987), packs this wealth of information into one, accessible paperback volume. Two other editions are recommended: F. Caudet (Madrid, 1983) and T. Tena (Mexico, 1975).

A history of translations into English marks the erratic interest taken in Galdós by Anglo-American readers. According to R. Russell, the only novels to appear in English before 1900 were a few of the first series, while at the turn of the century *Fortunata and Jacinta* remained unknown. No new translations appeared between 1895 and 1951. In 1961 *Fortunata and Jacinta* was translated into German, in 1970 into French, finally in 1973 into English (L. Clarke, London, 1973), followed much more successfully by A. Gullón's translation (Athens, GA, 1986). Currently available translations of Galdós's other novels are *Angel Guerra* (tr. K. Austin, Lewiston, NY, 1990), *Compassion* (tr. Juan Maclean, New York, 1966), *The Disinherited* (tr. L. Clarke, London, 1976), *Doña Perfecta* (tr. H. Onis, Great Neck, NY, 1960), *The Golden Fountain Café* (tr. W. Rubin, New York, 1989), *Marianela* (tr. H. Lester New York, 1960), *Miau* (tr. J.M. Cohen, Philadelphia, 1965), *Our Friend Manso* (tr. R. Russell, New York, 1987), *The Shadow* (tr. K. Austin, Athens, OH, 1980), *The Spendthrifts* (tr. G. Woolsey, London, 1962), *Torment* (tr. J.M. Cohen, London, 1952), *Torquemada in the Fire* (tr. N. Round, Glasgow, 1985), *Torquemada* (tr. F. López Morillas, New York, 1986), *Tristana* (tr. R.S. Rose, Peterborough, NH, 1961).

The manuscript of *Fortunata y Jacinta* (Span 93 (3) no. 65M-171) is housed in the Houghton Library, Harvard University (Cambridge, MA). The manuscript contains the novel in its entirety, as well as an incomplete, early version, penned on the back of several pages. Also at Harvard is the PhD dissertation (1972) of Diane Beth Hyman, "The *Fortunata y Jacinta* manuscript of Benito Pérez Galdós," which consists of a transcript of an earlier version of the novel.

Biography, letters, journalism

H. Chonon Berkowitz's *Pérez Galdós, Spanish Liberal Crusader* (Madison, 1948), remains the standard biography; a new biography by P. Ortiz Armengol is forthcoming. Two regional biographies, B. Madariaga's *Pérez Galdós. Biografía santanderina* (Santander, 1979) and A. Armas Ayala's *Galdós: lectura de una vida* (Santa Cruz de Tenerife, 1989) give accounts of Galdós's residence in Santander, beginning in 1871, and of visits to his native Canary Islands. L. Bonet's revised edition (Barcelona, 1990) of prologues, reviews, and speeches contains Galdós's most important essays. Letters from his contemporaries appear in three major collections: *Cartas a Galdós*. S. Ortega (Madrid, 1964), *Cartas del archivo de Galdós*, S. de la Nuez and J. Schraibman (Madrid, 1967), and *Cartas a Benito Pérez Galdós* (E. Pardo Bazán), C. Bravo Villasante (Madrid, 1975). Galdós's journalistic and other occasional writings have been edited by W. H. Shoemaker.

General studies, *Fortunata y Jacinta*

J. Casalduero's *Vida y obra de Galdós* (Madrid, 1943), a pioneering study that coincided with the centenary, adopts an historical and thematic approach. S. Eoff, *The Novels of Pérez Galdós* (St. Louis, 1954) gives a more conceptual, psychological interpretation. R. Gullón's *Galdós, novelista moderno* (Madrid, 1960) and J. F. Montesinos's three volume *Galdós* (Madrid, 1968–72) present the novels within comparative contexts. Gullón relates Galdós to Balzac, Dickens and Dostoevsky, while Montesinos focuses on Spanish literary antecedents.

G. Ribbans's seminal essay "Contemporary history in the structure and characterization of *Fortunata y Jacinta*," analyzes the interaction of history and fiction and provides the point of departure for P. Bly's *Galdós and the Novel of the Historical Imagination* (Liverpool, 1983). A. Andreu's *Galdós y la literatura popular* (Madrid, 1982) discusses Galdós's novel in the context of popular culture and R. Kirsner's *Años de Matrimonio en la novela de Galdós* (Eastchester, NY, 1983) treats at length the institution of marriage. B. Ciplijauskaité's *La mujer insatisfecha: El adulterio en la novela realista* (Galdós, Flaubert, Tolstoi, Caballero, James, Ibsen) (Barcelona, 1984), is a comparative study of the theme of adultery.

Important monographs on the contemporary social novels, with emphasis on *Fortunata and Jacinta* and the realism of Galdós, are M. Nimetz, *Humor in Galdós*, (New Haven, 1968), R. Gullón, *Técnicas de Galdós* (Madrid, 1970), J. Rodriguez Puértolas, *Galdós, burguesía y revolución* (Madrid, 1975), G. Ribbans's critical guide to *Fortunata y Jacinta* (London, 1977), K. Engler, *The Structure of Realism: the "Novelas Contemporáneas" of Benito Pérez Galdós* (Chapel Hill, NC, 1977), V. Chamberlin, *Galdós and Beethoven. 'Fortunata y Jacinta'. A Symphonic Novel* (London, 1977), S. Gilman, *Galdós and the Art of the European Novel, 1867–1887* (Princeton, 1981), D. Urey, *Galdós and the Irony of Language* (Cambridge, 1982), E. Rodgers, *From Enlightenment to Realism. The Novels of Galdós, 1870–1887* (Dublin, 1987) and A. Tsuchiya, *Images of the Sign. Semiotic Consciousness in the Novels of Benito Pérez Galdós* (Missouri University Press, 1990). Gullón's analyses initiate the corrective for those prevailing views of Galdós's "non-style," and Gilman's book reinstates Galdós among his European contemporaries. Rodgers offers perhaps the most balanced view of character, plot, and theme, as these evolve against the background of Spain's social and intellectual history. Rodgers also distinguishes among various theoretical approaches applied to Galdós's novels and follows Whiston and Ribbans in the emphasis on the importance of money and the "cash nexus." Rodgers's bibliography is indispensable.

Major collections of essays are: D. Rodgers, *Benito Pérez Galdós* (Madrid, 1973), J. Varey, *Galdós Studies I* (London, 1970), R. Weber, *Galdós Studies II* (London, 1974), P. Goldman, *Conflicting Realities: Four Readings of a Chapter by Pérez Galdós (Fortunata y Jacinta)*, part 3, chapter 4 (London, 1984), G. Gullón, *Fortunata y Jacinta* (Madrid, 1986), which reprints G. Sobejano's dense, resonant essay on Moreno-Isla, and P. Bly, *Galdós y la historia* (Ottawa Hispanic Studies 1, 1988).

The journal *Anales galdosianos* (1966–) contains C. Blanco Aguinaga's reply to S. Gilman, "On 'the birth of Fortunata'," (1968), S. Raphael's "Un extraño viaje de novios" (1968), A. Gullón's brilliant analysis of the bird-egg motif (1974) and J. Whiston's discussion of "half-conscious metaphors" (1972). Important essays in other publications are M. Hafter's study of ironic reprise, Anthony Zahareas, "The tragic sense in *Fortunata y Jacinta*," *Symposium* (1965), L. Braun's revisions of Guillermina Pacheco and Mauricia *la Dura*, R. Russell's analysis of Fortunata's speech (*Actas del Cuarto Congreso Internacional de Hispanistas*, 1982), J. Kronik's "Narraciones interiores en *Fortunata y Jacinta*," in *Homenaje a Juan López Morillas* (Madrid, 1982) and P. Goldman's discussion of Fortunata's rise from *pueblo* to middle class, ("Feijoo and Mr. Singer: notes on the *aburguesamiento* of Fortunata," *Revista de Estudios Hispánicos*-PR, 1982–84).

The papers of three interrelated symposia, convened to commemorate the centenary of the novel, have been collected and edited in separate volumes. Two have been published: *Revista La Torre*, 2, 1988; *Galdós. Centenario de 'Fortunata y Jacinta'* (1887–1987), edited by P. Palomo and J. Avila (Madrid, 1989); the third, *Textos y contextos de Galdós*, edited by J. Kronik and H. Turner, is forthcoming (Madrid, 1993). The papers discuss new theoretical approaches (N. Valis, J. Botrel), comparative contexts (J.P. Stern, G. Gullón), historical and social perspectives (P. Ortiz Armengol, C. Blanco Aguinaga), literary precedents (P. Palomo, L. Bonet), aspects of language (R. Russell, F. Caudet, A. Hernández Sein) and society (B. Ciplijauskaité, J.M. Navarro).

Printed in the United Kingdom
by Lightning Source UK Ltd.
106673UKS00001B/81